CLIMATE CHANGE

DISCOVER HOW IT IMPACTS SPACESHIP EARTH

Joshua Sneideman
and Erin Twamley

Illustrated by Mike Crosier

~ Latest titles in the *Build It Yourself* Series ~

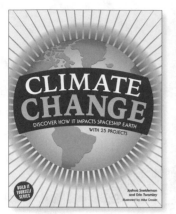

Check out more titles at www.nomadpress.net

Nomad Press
A division of Nomad Communications
10 9 8 7 6 5 4 3 2 1

This book was manufactured by Marquis Book Printing,
Montmagny Québec, Canada
April 2015, Job #112018

ISBN Softcover: 978-1-61930-273-0
ISBN Hardcover: 978-1-61930-269-3

Illustrations by Mike Crosier
Educational Consultant, Marla Conn

Questions regarding the ordering of this book should be addressed to
Nomad Press
2456 Christian St.
White River Junction, VT 05001
www.nomadpress.net

Printed in Canada.

CONTENTS

PS

Interested in primary sources?

Look for this icon. Use a smartphone or tablet app to scan the QR code and explore more about climate change! You can find a list of URLs on the Resources page.

TIMELINE

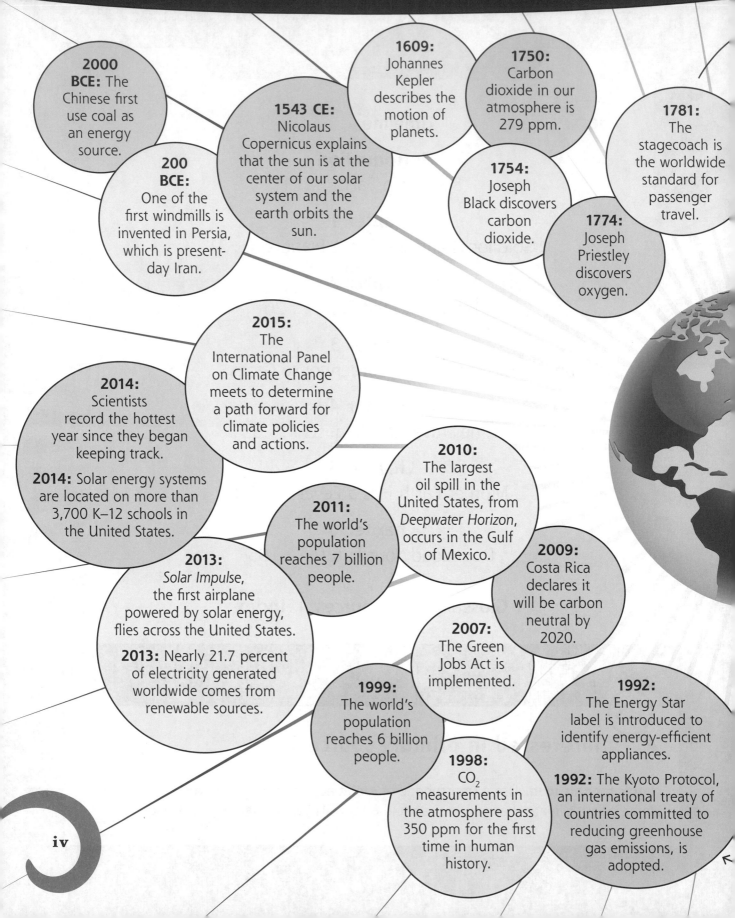

2000 BCE: The Chinese first use coal as an energy source.

200 BCE: One of the first windmills is invented in Persia, which is present-day Iran.

1543 CE: Nicolaus Copernicus explains that the sun is at the center of our solar system and the earth orbits the sun.

1609: Johannes Kepler describes the motion of planets.

1750: Carbon dioxide in our atmosphere is 279 ppm.

1754: Joseph Black discovers carbon dioxide.

1774: Joseph Priestley discovers oxygen.

1781: The stagecoach is the worldwide standard for passenger travel.

2015: The International Panel on Climate Change meets to determine a path forward for climate policies and actions.

2014: Scientists record the hottest year since they began keeping track.

2014: Solar energy systems are located on more than 3,700 K–12 schools in the United States.

2013: *Solar Impulse*, the first airplane powered by solar energy, flies across the United States.

2013: Nearly 21.7 percent of electricity generated worldwide comes from renewable sources.

2011: The world's population reaches 7 billion people.

2010: The largest oil spill in the United States, from *Deepwater Horizon*, occurs in the Gulf of Mexico.

2009: Costa Rica declares it will be carbon neutral by 2020.

2007: The Green Jobs Act is implemented.

1999: The world's population reaches 6 billion people.

1998: CO_2 measurements in the atmosphere pass 350 ppm for the first time in human history.

1992: The Energy Star label is introduced to identify energy-efficient appliances.

1992: The Kyoto Protocol, an international treaty of countries committed to reducing greenhouse gas emissions, is adopted.

TIMELINE

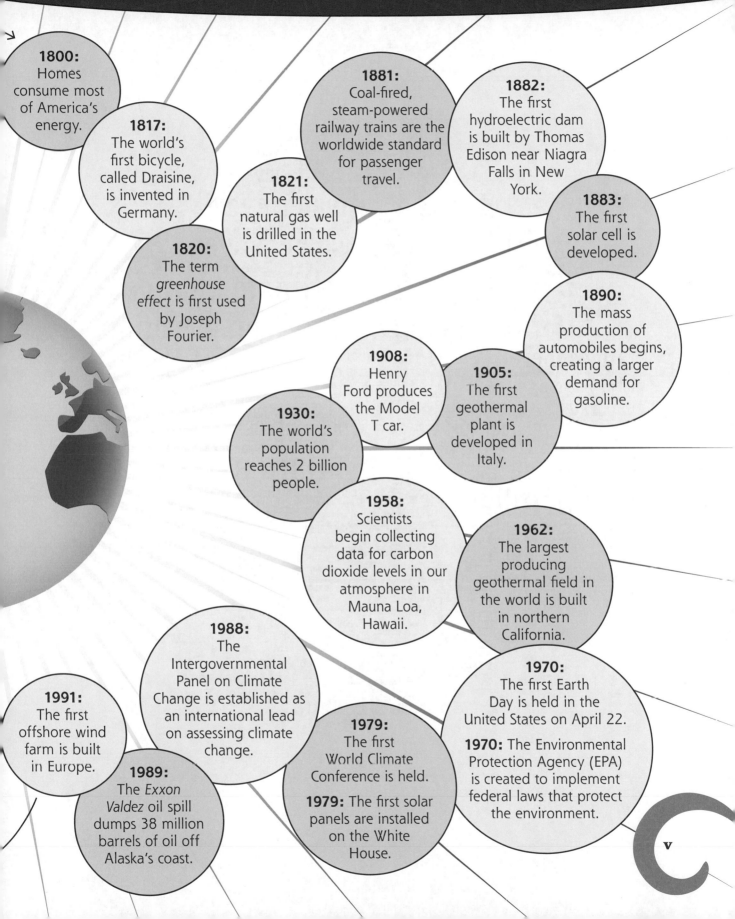

1800: Homes consume most of America's energy.

1817: The world's first bicycle, called Draisine, is invented in Germany.

1820: The term *greenhouse effect* is first used by Joseph Fourier.

1821: The first natural gas well is drilled in the United States.

1881: Coal-fired, steam-powered railway trains are the worldwide standard for passenger travel.

1882: The first hydroelectric dam is built by Thomas Edison near Niagra Falls in New York.

1883: The first solar cell is developed.

1890: The mass production of automobiles begins, creating a larger demand for gasoline.

1908: Henry Ford produces the Model T car.

1905: The first geothermal plant is developed in Italy.

1930: The world's population reaches 2 billion people.

1958: Scientists begin collecting data for carbon dioxide levels in our atmosphere in Mauna Loa, Hawaii.

1962: The largest producing geothermal field in the world is built in northern California.

1988: The Intergovernmental Panel on Climate Change is established as an international lead on assessing climate change.

1991: The first offshore wind farm is built in Europe.

1989: The *Exxon Valdez* oil spill dumps 38 million barrels of oil off Alaska's coast.

1979: The first World Climate Conference is held.

1979: The first solar panels are installed on the White House.

1970: The first Earth Day is held in the United States on April 22.

1970: The Environmental Protection Agency (EPA) is created to implement federal laws that protect the environment.

INTRODUCTION
SPACESHIP EARTH

Welcome aboard Spaceship Earth! Imagine our planet as a spaceship. Just as a spaceship carries everything its astronauts need to survive, our Spaceship Earth provides us with all the necessities for life.

When you watch a spaceship take off or look at photos of life inside a spacecraft, it's easy to see that the spaceship's **inhabitants** have to carry everything they need with them. There are no grocery stores or gas stations in space! Enough food, fuel, and water have to be brought on the spaceship for the duration of the flight. The ship also has **systems** to control both the temperature and the quality of the air, which have to be just right for the astronauts.

WORDS 2 KNOW

climate: the prevailing weather conditions of a region throughout the year, averaged over a series of years. These conditions include temperature, air pressure, humidity, precipitation, winds, sunshine, and cloudiness.

balance: when the different parts of something, such as in the environment or the climate, are distributed in the right amounts so that the whole system works and can keep working.

water cycle: the continuous movement of water from the earth to the clouds and back again.

climate change: a change in the long-term average weather patterns of a place.

atmosphere: the mixture of gases surrounding a planet.

By considering Earth as a spaceship, you can see how important it is to have freshwater to drink and clean air to breathe. It is our environment and our **climate** that make our home the way it is. Whether you live in hot, dry New Mexico or cool, rainy Oregon, you depend on the earth's systems to control the climate's delicate **balance**.

Most of the earth's systems are powered by the sun. The wind and **water cycles** bring rain that refills our freshwater sources while recycling the earth's fresh air supply. When the earth's systems become unbalanced, our planet experiences **climate change**.

COOL CONCEPT

The water cycle is the movement of water in a cycle between clouds, the land, oceans, and the **atmosphere**. A drop of water in the ocean may travel for more than 3,000 years before it falls as rain. Drops of water in the atmosphere may spend an average of eight days in the sky before falling back to the earth.

Metric Conversions

In the United States we use English measurements, but most scientists use metric measurements when performing experiments. To find the metric equivalents to the English measurements in this book, use the chart on page 118.

Climate change is the worldwide shift in the earth's normal weather patterns in response to human activity.

Have you noticed different weather patterns where you live? Have you heard about stronger, more frequent storms in the news? We experience climate change in many forms, from shorter winters and longer summers to changes in rainfall patterns and animal migration routes.

All of the earth's inhabitants have to **adapt** to the **impact** of climate change. Many scientists and citizens are working together to find solutions to our changing climate.

adapt: to change to survive in new or different conditions.

impact: an effect or influence.

natural resource: something found in nature that is useful to humans, such as water to drink, trees to burn, and fish to eat.

Take Care of Spaceship Earth

There are more than 7 billion people living on this planet using **natural resources** every day. We chop down trees for wood to build houses and burn for warmth. We use water to drink and bathe and wash dishes. We dig up gold and different metals to make jewelry, cars, and cell phones. How else do we affect the planet?

3

PS
Earth Selfies

Astronauts and satellites have been taking selfies of Earth for years.
Some show Earth within our **solar system** and others capture
Earth within the **universe**. What do you see most often in these pictures?

solar system: the collection of eight planets, moons, and other **celestial bodies** that **orbit** the sun.

celestial body: a star, planet, moon, or object in the sky.

orbit: a repeating path that circles around something else.

universe: everything that exists, everywhere.

nonrenewable: resources that can be used up, that we can't make more of, such as oil.

oxygen: a gas in the atmosphere that people and animals need to breathe to stay alive.

WORDS 2 KNOW

We also throw a lot of things away. From food and toys to packaging and clothes, we all produce waste. Americans produce an average of more than 4 pounds of waste a day. If you collected all the garbage produced in America during one year, you could fill up a line of garbage trucks all the way to the moon!

The more people on the planet, the more resources we use. But many of these resources are **nonrenewable** and will eventually run out. That is why it is very important we use our resources wisely. Our individual choices have an impact on the entire world.

Spaceship Earth's atmosphere surrounds our planet like a blanket. It gives us the **oxygen** we breathe and sustains life by moving oxygen around the planet. The atmosphere also controls the temperature on the surface of the earth.

For thousands of years, people thought of "air" as a single substance. They didn't know it was actually a mixture of gases. Can you name something else that is a mixture?

nitrogen: the most common gas in the earth's atmosphere.

carbon dioxide: a combination of carbon and oxygen that is formed by the burning of fossil fuels, the rotting of plants and animals, and the breathing out of animals or humans.

WORDS2KNOW

COOL CONCEPT

Our atmosphere is composed of many gases, but the most important to us are **nitrogen**, oxygen, and **carbon dioxide**. The levels of these gases must remain balanced in order for our atmosphere to continue to support life.

Changes to our atmosphere can have enormous consequences, including global climate change.

Measuring Change

In 1958, scientists at the Mauna Loa Observatory began sending up balloons off the coast of Hawaii to measure the carbon dioxide levels in our atmosphere. More than 50 years of measurements have been graphed on what is called the Keeling Curve. The curve is named after American scientist Charles David Keeling.

┌ GIANTS OF SCIENCE ┐

Charles David Keeling

Scientists used to think the oceans **absorbed** all the extra carbon dioxide from the atmosphere, but Charles David Keeling (1928–2005) had other ideas. He began measuring carbon dioxide levels in 1958 from Mauna Loa because it is located at a high **altitude**, far from any continent. This helped make sure the air that was sampled was mixed. The tracking of air samples during a long period of time has proved that the amount of carbon dioxide in our atmosphere is increasing.

absorb: to soak up.

altitude: the height of land above the level of the sea. Also called *elevation*.

fossil fuels: coal, oil, and natural gas. These energy sources come from the **fossils** of plants and **microorganisms** that lived millions of years ago.

fossil: the remains or traces of ancient plants or animals left in rock.

microorganism: a living thing that is so small it can be seen only with a microscope. Also called a microbe.

WORDS 2 KNOW

Dr Keeling discovered a way to measure carbon dioxide in the atmosphere. The measurements on the curve named after him demonstrate that the levels of carbon dioxide in our atmosphere are increasing.

There are many different reasons for the increase in carbon dioxide in the atmosphere. Many human activities produce carbon dioxide, including burning **fossil fuels** and forests. All animals, including humans, release carbon dioxide into the atmosphere when they breathe.

This means a growing population creates more carbon dioxide.

Scientists study climate change by making observations, gathering **data** through **scientific inquiry**, and thinking creatively and critically about different **theories**. What impact do humans have on the environment? What happens when we damage it? How does this affect our climate? Scientists ask these questions, the same ones that we will look at in this book.

We need to take care of Earth, just as we'd take care of a spaceship, so that it can take care of us!

data: information, usually measured in the form of numbers, that can be processed by a computer.

scientific inquiry: an approach to teaching and learning science based on questions, experiments, and evaluation of data.

theory: an explanation of how or why something happens that is accepted to be true.

WORDS 2 KNOW

Good Science Practices

Every good scientist keeps a science journal! Scientists use the scientific method to keep their experiments organized. Choose a notebook to use as your science journal. As you read through this book and do the activities, keep track of your observations and record each step in a scientific method worksheet, like the one shown here.

Each chapter of this book begins with an essential question to help guide your exploration of climate change.

Question: What are we trying to find out? What problem are we trying to solve?

Research: What do other people think?

Hypothesis/Prediction: What do we think the answer will be?

Equipment: What supplies are we using?

Method: What procedure are we following?

Results: What happened and why?

? ESSENTIAL QUESTION

Keep the question in your mind as you read the chapter. At the end of each chapter, use your science journal to record your thoughts and answers.

IDEAS FOR SUPPLIES
*ice * cooking pot * timer * thermometer*

The water cycle plays a major role in our earth's climate. It both stores and transfers energy from the sun. In the water cycle, water changes from a solid to a liquid to a gas, back and forth, over and over again. Can you name some solids, liquids, and gases?

During the water cycle, bodies of water such as lakes and oceans absorb the sun's energy. Some of the water **evaporates**. When **water vapor** enters the atmosphere, it cools or **condenses** into droplets. During condensation, the droplets become clouds. When the water droplets become heavy enough, they fall as rain or snow, depending on the temperature. This is called **precipitation**. How do you think melting and freezing fits into the water cycle?

As you use the scientific method to make observations and collect data, trust your data and make observations without judgment. Your thermometer is not broken! **Caution: Ask an adult to supervise the boiling of water.**

evaporate: when a liquid heats up and changes into a gas.

water vapor: water as a gas, such as fog, steam, or mist.

WORDS 2 KNOW

condense: when a gas cools down and changes into a liquid.

precipitation: condensed water vapor that falls to the earth's surface in the form of rain, snow, sleet, or hail.

1 Create a data table in your science journal like the one on the next page. Use this table to record your observations and make connections to your own life experiences.

2 Start a scientific method worksheet like the one on page 7. Make a prediction for the temperature at which water will change from solid to liquid and from liquid to gas. This is your hypothesis.

	Prediction At what temperature do you think the phase change will occur?	Observation Actual temperature when phase change occurred.	Connection Where have you observed this change in your own life?
Solid			
Liquid			
Gas			

3 Fill a pot halfway with ice and set a timer for 3 minutes. Observe and record the temperature every 60 seconds. Be careful not to touch the bottom of the pot with the thermometer.

4 Place the pot on the stove over medium heat. Stir slowly. Don't heat the ice too quickly.

5 As you stir, continue to record temperature data every 60 seconds until 3 minutes after the water has reached a rolling boil. Once the water begins to boil, have an adult take over stirring. A liquid is at a rolling boil when it boils continuously, even when you are stirring it.

TRY THIS: Make a graph using your temperature data, with the temperature on the y axis and the time intervals on the x axis. What is a good title for your graph? When you connect the dots after plotting your temperature data points, do you see a pattern? Record these observations in your scientific method worksheet.

Ask your parents' permission to use these websites to create your own charts and graphs. Cover up neighboring QR codes to make sure you're scanning the right one! Why are charts and graphs easier to read?

BUILD A BALANCE BOARD

**Earth's atmosphere is in a delicate balance. Humans are
adding carbon dioxide at a rapid rate. The atmosphere
needs to stay in balance just like your balance board,
but it doesn't take much to create an imbalance.**

1 Try balancing your flat object on your round object. What happens?

2 Place similar objects on each side of
the board and try to balance them. Add
complexity by trying different objects on
different sides. What happens?

THINK ABOUT IT:

Was it easy or hard to balance
your objects? What happens
if you use a different round
object under the flat object?
What does this show you about
our atmosphere's
balancing act? What
happens if our
atmosphere is out
of balance?

CHAPTER 1
GOLDILOCKS AND THE THREE PLANETS

Remember the story of Goldilocks and the three bears? A little girl named Goldilocks sneaks into the bears' home and tries to find food that's not too hot and not too cold, a chair that's not too big and not too small, and a bed that's not too hard and not too soft. She is looking for things that are just right.

Scientists who study planets can relate to the story of Goldilocks as they explore the universe with their powerful telescopes, looking for places where life might exist. These planetary scientists examine whether a planet is too hot or too cold, too big or too small, and whether the atmosphere is too thin or too thick for life to exist. They are hoping to find planets where conditions are just right for liquid water to exist. Planetary scientists call these planets "Goldilocks planets."

? ESSENTIAL QUESTION

How do scientists know if a planet is a Goldilocks planet? What do they measure to find out?

If a planet orbits too closely to its sun, it will be too hot. If the planet orbits too far away, it will be too cold. The area where an orbit is just right is called the **habitable zone**. A planet in the habitable zone won't be too hot or too cold. It will be just right.

Planets that are too small don't have enough gravity to maintain an atmosphere. They cool too quickly for life to exist. A planet that is too big, such as Jupiter, the largest planet in our solar system, has no land. It is made of mostly gas and ice.

Earth is a Goldilocks planet. Conditions are just right for water to exist as a solid, liquid, and gas. Astronauts have described the earth as the blue planet. Images from space show that nearly 71 percent of the planet is covered by bodies of water.

Should we call it planet Water instead of planet Earth?

habitable zone: the region at a distance from a star where liquid water is likely to exist.

rotation: turning around a fixed point.

elliptical: shaped like an ellipse, or an oval.

WORDS 2 KNOW

GIANTS OF SCIENCE

Johannes Kepler

How do we know about the orbits of planets? We can credit planetary scientists, including Johannes Kepler (1571–1630), who have observed planets and their **rotation** through telescopes. Before Kepler proved otherwise, people thought planets orbited the sun in perfect circles, but Kepler discovered that the orbits of planets are actually **elliptical**. NASA named the space telescope used to hunt planets after Kepler. The Kepler Space Telescope has discovered more than 1,000 planets since it was first launched in 2009.

All features of Venus, except one, are named after women. All features of Mars, except one, are named after men. All of the planets in our solar system, except Earth, are named after Roman gods and goddesses.

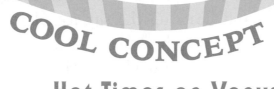

COOL CONCEPT

Hot Times on Venus

Get up before daylight or stay out after sunset and you can often see Venus in the sky. Venus is the brightest object in the night sky after the moon. It looks like a bright, yellowish star. Venus is the second-closest planet to the sun, after Mercury, and the hottest planet in our solar system. How hot is Venus? Even metal will melt on this planet!

Some people think Venus is extremely hot because of its proximity to the sun, but the real reason Venus is so hot is its super-thick atmosphere. Venus is covered in clouds so thick that almost no heat escapes back to space. The **heat-trapping gas** carbon dioxide makes up 96 percent of Venus's atmosphere.

heat-trapping gas: a gas, such as carbon dioxide, water vapor, or **methane**, that absorbs and stores heat.

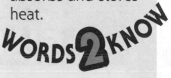

methane: a **greenhouse gas** that is colorless and odorless, composed of carbon and hydrogen.

greenhouse gas: a gas in the atmosphere that traps heat. We need some greenhouse gases, but too many trap too much heat.

13

Have you ever gotten into a car that has been parked in the sun on a summer day? What's it like inside?

Sunlight enters through the glass windows and heats up the surface of the materials in the car, such as the seats and dashboard. Heat can't pass through the glass as easily as light because it vibrates at a different **wavelength**. The heat's waves are **infrared**. The air inside the car gets hotter and hotter, and when you open the door to the car several hours after leaving it, you encounter very high heat!

Venus is just like the car. Light gets in, heats the surface of the planet, and the heat can't get back out again.

GIANTS OF SCIENCE

Carl Sagan

Planetary scientist Carl Sagan (1934–1996) was the first scientist to correctly explain the mystery of the high temperatures of Venus as a massive **greenhouse effect**. Sagan fell in love with astronomy as a child when he learned that every star in the night sky was a distant sun. He helped NASA's *Apollo 11* astronauts before their flights to the moon, and helped design NASA's *Mariner*, *Viking*, *Voyager*, and *Galileo* missions.

The heat has nowhere to go because the atmosphere, like the glass windows of a car, won't allow the heat to escape. The carbon dioxide in Venus's atmosphere prevents the heat from leaving the planet. This is known as the greenhouse effect. We are experiencing a similar effect on Earth. As the amount of carbon dioxide increases in the earth's atmosphere, more heat gets trapped at the surface and the temperature of the planet rises. This contributes to the earth's changing climate.

Here on Earth, people use greenhouses to grow food, especially during the winter. Why do you think this works?

Scientists describe the extreme temperature of Venus as a "runaway greenhouse effect." They say it is running away because the atmosphere heats up to such a high degree that it never cools down again.

Extreme Living

Extremophiles are small **organisms** that can live in some of the most extreme conditions. They live where most humans cannot go. Extremophiles can be found in the super-heated waters of the ocean floor near heat vents, in the extreme saltiness of the Dead Sea, in the freezing cold of Antarctica, and even in the driest deserts on the planet. They provide us with clues that life may survive in some of the most unexpected places. Maybe even on the super-heated surface of Venus!

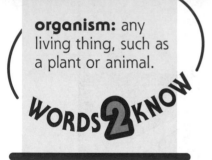

organism: any living thing, such as a plant or animal.

WORDS 2 KNOW

The super-hot temperatures and thick clouds on Venus make it hard for scientists to study its surface. The planet remains little explored and hidden in mystery. In 1982, an unmanned Russian spacecraft landed on Venus and sent some beautiful color images back to Earth. About two hours after landing on the surface, the spacecraft was destroyed by the extreme heat.

Is Venus a Goldilocks planet? Is it just right?

Cold Times on Mars

Scientists know more about Mars, which is sometimes called the red planet because of its reddish color, than they do about Venus. In fact, scientists know more about the surface of Mars than we do about the floors of our very own oceans!

The atmosphere of Mars is very thin, and this is part of the reason we know so much about this planet. It allows us to clearly see the surface. We use telescopes and rovers, which are car-sized, remote-controlled space exploration vehicles, to collect data and take pictures on the surfaces of planets.

The thin atmosphere of the planet also affects the temperature of Mars. Light from the sun enters the atmosphere, bounces off the surface, and leaves, allowing very little time for the planet to warm up.

If Venus is like a car with its windows rolled up, Mars is more like a bicycle. Mars allows all of its heat to escape back into space. Is Mars a Goldilocks planet? Why or why not?

Planet	Average Surface Temperature
Mars	-80 degrees Fahrenheit (-62 degrees Celsius)
Earth	57.2 degrees Fahrenheit (14 degrees Celsius)
Venus	864 degrees Fahrenheit (462 degrees Celsius)

COOL CONCEPT

The moon has no atmosphere to trap heat from the sun, so the moon is one of the hottest places in the solar system during the day and one of the coldest at night.

GIANTS OF SCIENCE

Colette Lohr

Colette Lohr is an engineer and strategic mission officer with NASA who helps operate the Mars rover *Curiosity*. Operating *Curiosity* is a big job, taking nearly 90 people a day to make sure it doesn't break down. Lohr established Women's Curiosity Day on June 26, 2014, to highlight the role of women in science. On this day, women took over almost all the rover support jobs.

element: a substance whose **atoms** are all the same. Examples include gold, oxygen, nitrogen, and carbon.

atom: the smallest particle of an element.

molecule: a group of atoms bound together to form a new substance. Examples include carbon dioxide (CO_2), one carbon atom and two oxygen atoms, and water (H_2O), two **hydrogen** atoms and one oxygen atom.

hydrogen: the simplest and most abundant element in the universe.

WORDS 2 KNOW

NASA has been exploring Mars since its first successful mission to Mars in 1964, when *Mariner 4* took 21 pictures of the surface. Since then, the United States has successfully launched 18 missions to Mars. NASA also uses rovers to take pictures, perform experiments, and collect data.

Earth—the Goldilocks Planet

If Goldilocks were choosing planets, she would choose Earth—its atmosphere is just right. Sunlight enters the atmosphere and generates heat, but the right balance of **elements** and **molecules** prevents all that heat from being trapped. Just enough escapes so that liquid water, and life, can exist on Earth. All of these characteristics help create a climate that can support life.

One way to think about atmosphere is by comparison. Venus's atmosphere is 100 times thicker than Earth's atmosphere, and 12,150 times thicker than Mars's. The thicker the atmosphere, the greater the number of heat-trapping molecules. Since Venus's atmosphere is very thick, Venus is a very hot planet.

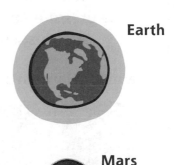

Venus

Earth

Mars

As you'll read in the following chapters, there are plenty of things you can do to make sure the greenhouse effect does not run away on Earth. In the next chapter, we will explore how climate and life are connected to the sun.

Why does one planet in our solar system have an abundance of life while the others appear to have no life?

Consider the Essential Question

Write your thoughts about this chapter's Essential Question in your science journal, using information you've gathered from reading and knowledge you may already have. Share it with other students and friends. Did you all come up with the same answers? What is different? Do this for every chapter.

?

ESSENTIAL QUESTION

How do scientists know if a planet is a Goldilocks planet? What do they measure to find out?

MAKE A CAN CRUSHER

*ice water * empty soda can * saucepan * oven mitts * cooking tongs*

Is an empty soda can really empty? It might not have any soda in it, but it is full of air. The earth's atmosphere pushes in all directions— it's inside the can pushing out and it's outside the can pushing in. The pressure pushing out is in balance with the pressure pushing in. What happens if we create a vacuum inside the can, making the pressure on the outside greater than the pressure on the inside? Start a scientific method worksheet in your science journal.

Caution: Have an adult help you with the hot can.

1 Fill a saucepan with ice water and set it aside.

vacuum: a space that is empty.

recyclable: something that can be recycled by shredding, squashing, pulping, or melting to use the materials to create new products.

WORDS 2 KNOW

2 Pour 1 tablespoon of water into an empty soda can. Use oven mitts and cooking tongs to heat the can on the stove. Boil the water until a cloud of steam escapes from the opening in the can.

3 Quickly flip the can upside down into the ice water saucepan. What happens?

THINK ABOUT IT: Why is compacting **recyclables** and other waste a good idea?

COOL CONCEPT

20

Earth's air pressure is 135 times greater than the air pressure on Mars. What would happen to the empty soda can on the surface of Venus or on the surface of Mars?

Use your imagination to travel to extreme planets!

1 Thinking about the differences between Venus, Mars, and Earth, draw yourself exploring each planet.

Below are some things to think about.

* What would someone wear to explore each planet?

* What special equipment would you need to survive?

* How long could someone stay?

* What color is each planet?

Carbon Dioxide on Your Planet

Earth, Mars, and Venus all have carbon dioxide in their atmospheres. Even though Mars and Venus both have about the same percent of carbon dioxide, they have very different temperatures. Why?

Planet	Carbon Dioxide	Oxygen	Nitrogen
Earth	less than 0.04 percent	21 percent	78 percent
Mars	95 percent	less than 1 percent	2.7 percent
Venus	96 percent	less than 1 percent	3.5 percent

MAKE A TELESCOPE

A telescope is a **scientific instrument** that helps us see faraway objects such as planets and stars. Telescopes use a pair of special **lenses**. An objective lens collects light from a distant object. An eyepiece lens refocuses the light to allow you to see the object. Telescopes come in various sizes and with different lenses. You can create your own simple telescope to explore the moon.

1 Neatly tape the edges of the smaller magnifying glass lens to one end of the smaller cardboard tube. This will be your eyepiece.

scientific instrument: a tool or device used in science experiments.

lens: a clear, curved piece of glass or plastic that is used in eyeglasses, cameras, and telescopes to make things look clearer or bigger.

WORDS 2 KNOW

2 Neatly tape your larger lens to the end of the larger cardboard tube. This is your objective lens, which collects light from the object the telescope is pointed at and beams it to the eyepiece. It magnifies that light enough so your eye can see the object.

3 Try out your refracting telescope by pointing it at a piece of printed paper across the room. Adjust the cardboard tubes with one inside the other to change the focus. Can you make all the writing clear enough to read through your telescope?

4 Take your telescope outside at night and look at the moon. What can you see? With an adult's permission, find a map of the moon online so you can identify the areas you spot through your telescope. Draw your own map of the moon and label all the areas you can see with your telescope.

TRY THIS: Try finding star clusters in the sky. Research online to discover the names of these stars, and keep track of what you see in the nighttime sky in your science journal.

Exploring Mars

How do we know so much about Mars? Many rovers have been sent to Mars to study the surface and atmosphere. **Check out the video of *Curiosity* and how it landed on Mars using new technology.**

To help explore how climate and atmosphere may be changing on Mars, NASA launched *MAVEN* (Mars Atmospheric and Volatile Evolution) to explore Mars's atmosphere. *MAVEN* is the first spacecraft mission dedicated to exploring the upper atmosphere of Mars. **Watch *MAVEN* orbit Mars.**

BUILD A SOLAR COOKER

IDEAS FOR SUPPLIES
*empty pizza box * aluminum foil * black construction paper * newspaper * clear plastic wrap * something to heat up, such as cold pizza*

Light from the sun can be used to cook food! A solar oven can be used to heat up a piece of pizza or make s'mores, but it won't get hot enough to burn you or bake things. Be sure to have an adult help you.

1 Make sure the pizza box is folded into its box shape and closed.

2 Trace the outline of a piece of notebook paper in the center of the box lid.

3 Carefully cut along three edges of the rectangle that you just traced on the lid of the box to form a flap of cardboard. Gently fold the flap back along the uncut edge to make a crease.

4 Wrap the inside of this flap with aluminum foil. Tape it on the outside to hold it firmly. Try to keep the tape from showing on the inside of the flap. The foil will help to reflect the sunlight into the box.

5 Open the box and place a piece of black construction paper on the bottom of the box. This will help your oven absorb the sun's heat.

6 Roll up newspaper into 1½-inch-thick rolls. Fit them around the inside edges of the box and secure with tape. This insulation will help hold in the sun's heat.

Tape plastic wrap here

Tape plastic wrap here

7 Cut two pieces of plastic wrap an inch larger than the flap opening. Tape one piece of plastic wrap to the underside of the flap, over the foil. After taping one side, be sure to pull the plastic wrap tight, and tape down all four sides so the plastic is sealed against the foil.

8 Tape the other piece of plastic wrap over the flap opening. Again, be sure the plastic wrap is tight and tape down all four edges to form a seal. Why is this important? How is the plastic wrap acting like an atmosphere?

PIZZA PIZZA

Pizza goes here

9 Place a piece of cold pizza in the box in the sun. Open the flap and turn the box so the foil is facing the sun. Move the flap up and down and note how it reflects the sunlight.

10 Use a ruler or stick to prop up the flap so that it bounces the sunlight into the box, right on the pizza. Wait about a half hour for the box to warm up in the sun. Enjoy your warmed-up treat!

TAKE IT FURTHER: Can you use your solar oven if it is cold outside? Place a towel or blanket under the box so the bottom doesn't get cold. Set up the oven in the same way. Did your oven get just as hot as in the summer?

CHAPTER 2
BITING INTO THE SUN

What did you have for breakfast this morning? Eggs and toast? Cereal and orange juice? An apple with peanut butter? The sun is responsible for the energy in everything you ate for breakfast. This is because the sun is the primary source of energy in every ecosystem.

Did you have milk for breakfast? Milk comes from cows, and cows get their energy by eating grass and grain. Plants use sunlight to make sugar from carbon dioxide and water. This sugar, which is stored in the plant's cells, is the source of energy for almost all **food chains**. Most life, including the cow that made your milk, can trace the energy in their food back to the sun. When you bite into an apple, you are biting into the sun!

? ESSENTIAL QUESTION

How does the sun affect the earth?
Could we have life without the sun?

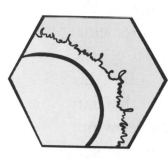

As you bite into your delicious apple, you have the sun to thank for the energy it provides your body. The sun's light powers all of the earth's systems. The sun gives us light and heat. Without it, the earth would be a cold, dark place that could not support life. Could the apple grow in deep space, where the sun doesn't shine and the temperature is -270 degrees Fahrenheit (-168 degrees Celsius)?

The sun's energy is trapped by gases in the atmosphere. This trapped energy remains in the earth's atmosphere, warming the planet.

Is the sun causing climate change? NASA scientists and satellites have been studying the sun for decades. Data collected shows that the sun's energy is released in a regular pattern. Since 1950, the sun's energy has not changed to have any impact on the increase of the earth's temperature.

So what is causing the earth to heat up? Scientists and citizens agree that humanity's demand for energy is causing climate change. We need energy for everything from growing food to building skyscrapers. For more than 100 years, we have been burning fossil fuels that release carbon dioxide into the atmosphere. This is what is causing **global warming**.

Do we need to burn fossil fuels? Could we tap into the power of the sun for the energy we need instead?

global warming: an increase in the average temperature of the earth's atmosphere.

WORDS 2 KNOW

renewable energy: a form of energy that doesn't get used up, including the energy of the sun and the wind.

biofuel: fuel made from living matter, such as plants.

mass: the amount of matter in an object.

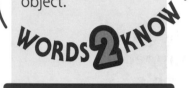

The sun's energy may be one of the solutions to our climate change problems. The sun is responsible for most of the **renewable energy** on Earth. In this chapter, we will explore the role the sun plays in renewable energy, which includes wind, water, and **biofuels**. You will see how the sun drives the earth's systems, including climate, and is critical to life on Earth.

In one day the earth receives more energy from the sun than the world uses in one year!

What Is a Sun?

Our sun is a star that is 4.6 billion years old. It shares similarities with all the other stars in the night sky, except the sun is at the center of our solar system and the other stars are much farther away. This is why the sun looks so big when all the other stars look so small. The sun is our solar system's largest object, containing 99 percent of all its **mass**. In fact, 1.3 million Earths could fit into the sun!

COOL CONCEPT

Deep in the ocean where the sun never shines lives a type of organism that can make its own food without sunlight. These creatures, called chemosynthetic organisms, convert chemicals and heat into sugar. They get heat from vents in the floor of the ocean.

The Color of the Sun

Draw a picture of the sun. What color do you use? Although the sun appears to be yellow to the human eye, it's actually white. White is a mixture of all the colors of the rainbow. When light from the sun goes through our atmosphere, those colors are separated and scattered. Blue and violet light spreads out to make the color of the sky, while the yellows, oranges, and reds stick around to make the sun look yellow.

What is the sun made of? Very hot gases! The sun is mostly hydrogen gas (91 percent) and **helium** gas (8 percent). At the sun's **core**, hydrogen is **compressed**, which makes it very hot.

The temperature in the sun's core is more than 10 million degrees Fahrenheit (5,555,538 degrees Celsius). That is more than 12,000 times hotter than Venus! These high temperatures cause the hydrogen atoms to combine and form helium in a **nuclear reaction** known as **fusion**. Fusion is the source of the sun's energy.

More than 10,000,000 degrees Fahrenheit

helium: a light gas often used to fill balloons. It is the most abundant element after hydrogen.

WORDS 2 KNOW

core: the center of an object.

compress: to squeeze a material very tightly.

nuclear reaction: when atoms fuse together or split apart. This releases a large amount of energy.

fusion: when the **nucleus** of one atom combines with the nucleus of another atom, which releases energy.

nucleus: the center of an atom. Plural is nuclei.

29

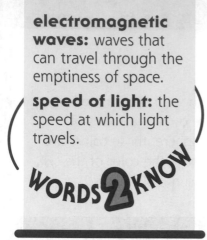

electromagnetic waves: waves that can travel through the emptiness of space.

speed of light: the speed at which light travels.

How does energy from the sun reach the earth from more than 93 million miles away? The sun's energy travels in **electromagnetic waves**. The word *electromagnetic* means the waves are both electric and magnetic. They move continuously by pushing and pulling on electric and magnetic fields.

All electromagnetic waves travel at the **speed of light**, which is 186,000 miles per second (299,338 kilometers per second). That is the same as traveling around the equator of the earth 7.5 times in one second. Sunlight takes 8 minutes and 20 seconds to reach the earth at the speed of light.

If the sun were to magically disappear right now, how long would it take you to know it was gone?

Orbit and Tilt

The earth makes one complete trip around the sun every 365.25 days. This is called the earth's revolution, and it's how we measure a year. The earth's path around the sun, its orbit, is in the shape of an ellipse, or an oval.

Every four years we have a leap year. Leap years are when we add February 29th to the calendar. We do this because the earth's revolution around the sun takes a quarter day more than 365 days.

COOL CONCEPT

hemisphere: half of the earth. Above the equator is called the Northern Hemisphere and below is the Southern Hemisphere.

WORDS 2 KNOW

Scientists think of the earth as being divided in half at the equator, into two **hemispheres**. The top half is called the Northern Hemisphere and the bottom half is the Southern Hemisphere.

When it's winter in the Northern Hemisphere, it's summer in the Southern Hemisphere. That means when someone in Boston is having fun playing in the snow, someone in Australia is swimming at the beach. What causes the change in seasons, and why are the seasons different around the world?

GIANTS OF SCIENCE

Nicolaus Copernicus

Nicolaus Copernicus lived in Royal Prussia from 1473 to his death in 1543. His work changed how people viewed their place in our solar system. For thousands of years, humans believed the earth was the center of the universe and the sun and planets orbited the earth. In 1543, Copernicus published a book that explained the sun was in the center and the earth and planets rotated around the sun.

axis: the imaginary line through the North and South Poles that the earth rotates around.

WORDS2KNOW

The earth does not rotate around the sun standing straight up. Instead, it's tilted on its **axis**. This 23.5-degree tilt of the earth is the reason for our changing seasons.

The Northern Hemisphere experiences summer when it is tilted toward the sun. The Northern Hemisphere's winter happens when it is tilted away from the sun. This movement around the sun causes a change in the amount and strength of the sunlight that reaches the surface of the planet.

In summer, the days are longer and the sunlight is more concentrated because you're tilted toward the sun. In the winter, the days are shorter and colder because the sun's rays are less concentrated.

PS

Having a Looooong Day?

Are days and nights always the same length? How many hours of daylight do you have in a day during the winter? During the summer? That number will depend on where you live. The closer you are to the equator, the less change there is in the amount of daylight. Enter your own location on this website to see a graph of changing hours of daylight for your area.

Sunspots

As early as 28 BCE, humans noticed dark spots on the sun. These sunspots can be seen through telescopes. The spots are actually cooler magnetic areas on the sun that appear in 11-year cycles. Sunspots help scientists study **trends** and patterns in space to better understand the solar system, from meteorites to temperature changes. Scientists on Earth who have compared the history of sunspots to temperature data on Earth have found that sunspots have been present in both cold and warm temperature time periods. This shows that there is no connection between sunspots and climate change on Earth.

Weather or Not?

Not only does the earth's relationship to the sun create our seasons, but the sun also impacts weather and climate.

Weather is the conditions that occur during a few hours or days. We usually describe it based on amounts of sunlight, precipitation, and temperature. Climate can be described as the average weather during a period of more than 30 years.

If you live in Arizona, your climate is dry and hot. The weather may include thunderstorms or rain. When scientists study the trends and patterns in climate change they are looking at patterns across many years. These patterns can be found in temperature data or frequency of natural events such as thunderstorms and wildfires. Scientists say that climate change in Arizona will lead to increased temperatures, wildfires, and **drought**.

WORDS 2 KNOW

trend: a particular direction or path.

drought: a long period of time without rain.

33

Can you guess the coldest place on Earth? If you guessed a spot in Antarctica you are right! Vostok Station holds the record with -128.6 degrees Fahrenheit (-89.2 degrees Celsius) in 1983 in July! Compare that to the hottest place on Earth, Death Valley, California, where a temperature of 134 degrees Fahrenheit (56.7 degrees Celsius) has been recorded. What is the temperature difference between these two locations?

COOL CONCEPT

photoelectric effect: the creation of an electric current after exposure to light.

solar power: energy from the sun converted to electricity.

WORDS 2 KNOW

Climate change affects different places in different ways. For example, the temperatures at the North Pole are rising faster than anywhere on Earth. The temperatures at the South Pole are not changing as fast. Mountain areas will be affected differently than coastal areas. Deserts will be impacted differently than rainforests.

No matter where you live, however, the earth as a whole is getting warmer.

GIANTS OF SCIENCE

Albert Einstein

Albert Einstein is one of the greatest scientists of all time. His 1905 discovery of the **photoelectric effect** was important for the development of solar panels. Without his discovery, we would not be able to produce **solar power**. In 1921, Einstein received a Nobel Prize in physics for this work.

Renewable Energy From the Sun

solar panel: a device used to capture sunlight and convert it to usable energy.

WORDS2KNOW

Renewable energy from the sun is all around us. Using renewable energy reduces the amount of carbon dioxide released in the air, and renewable energy technologies are less harmful to our environment. Renewable energy from the sun can be captured using **solar panels**.

The first home with solar panels in the United States was built in 1948 in Massachusetts by two women. Physicist Dr. Mária Telkes and architect Eleanor Raymond teamed up to build a house with a solar panel roof. This house proved that even in cold climates such as that in Massachusetts, the sun's energy can power a house. Dr. Telkes was known as the "Sun Queen" in the early twentieth century for all of her solar-powered inventions, including solar ovens and water-cleaning systems powered by the sun.

Element Symbols

Each element has a symbol, and when mixtures are made of those elements, their symbols tell us the number of atoms of each element in the mixture. This chart shows some common elements found in our atmosphere. Methane has one atom of carbon and four atoms of hydrogen. How many atoms of oxygen does carbon dioxide have?

Element	Symbol
nitrogen	N
oxygen	O
hydrogen	H
carbon	C
carbon dioxide	CO_2
methane	CH_4

dense: how tightly the matter in an object is packed.

atmospheric pressure: the weight of all the air pressing down on an area.

convection current: the movement of hot air rising and cold air sinking.

WORDS 2 KNOW

Renewable Energy From Wind, Water, and Plants

Have you ever been at the beach on a hot day and felt a cool breeze come off the ocean? You can thank the sun! The sun heats the air over land more quickly than it heats the air over the ocean. As the air over the land gets hot, it rises, because warm air rises and cold air sinks. Warm air is less **dense** and lighter than cold air.

The rising warm air leaves what's called low **atmospheric pressure**. The cooler air from over the ocean, where there's high atmospheric pressure, rushes in to try to balance the pressure. We feel this **convection current** as wind! If you've ever seen a windmill, you've seen the wind's energy captured to generate electricity.

The first solar panels on the White House were installed under President Jimmy Carter in 1979.

COOL CONCEPT

algae: a plant-like organism that turns light into energy. Algae does not have leaves or roots.

WORDS 2 KNOW

The sun is also responsible for the power we generate from water. Energy from the sun warms the water, causing it to evaporate, turn into clouds, and come back to the earth as precipitation. This is the water cycle. Without the sun, rain and snow would not fall and rivers would not flow. Dams and other technologies convert the energy of water into electricity.

New Zealand generates more than 50 percent of its electricity from moving water.

Biofuels are another alternative energy source. Switch grass, sugar cane, sugar beets, **algae**, and more can be pressed into a liquid fuel. These biofuels can run our cars, trucks, planes, and boats. The U.S. military is the largest user of biofuel in the world.

The sun provides energy for plants to grow and the food animals eat. We can capture its energy to create heat and electricity for our homes and fuels for our cars. From the tiniest organisms to the largest animals, all life relies on the sun for survival.

Biting into the sun and using its clean renewable energy is our best chance for a cleaner atmosphere. Solar, wind, water, and wave energy can be converted into electricity without releasing a single molecule of carbon dioxide. Now that's clean! In the next chapter, we explore the balance of carbon dioxide and other gases in the atmosphere and the effect of this balance on the climate.

? ESSENTIAL QUESTION

Now it's time to consider and discuss the Essential Question:
How does the sun affect the earth? Could we have life without the sun?

BUILD YOUR OWN SUNDIAL

IDEAS FOR SUPPLIES
*paper plate * drawing materials * plastic straw * pushpins*

How do you tell time? The oldest clock and first scientific instrument was a sundial. Created by Egyptians and used throughout history and even today in many parts of the world, sundials come in all shapes, sizes, and materials. Build your own sundial and mark the change in the sun's shadow to create a timepiece. For best results, do this project on a sunny day.

1 Punch a hole in the center of a paper plate. Don't make the hole bigger than the straw. You want the straw to fit snugly into the hole so it stands up straight.

2 Draw the number "12" on any edge of your plate. Draw a line from the number to the center hole. Use a ruler to keep the line straight!

3 At noon, stick your half straw into the hole in the plate and put the plate on the ground. Slowly turn the plate until the shadow of the straw falls on the line to number 12. Secure the sundial to the ground with some pushpins.

4 Where do you think the shadow of the straw will be at 1 p.m., 2 p.m., 3 p.m., and beyond? Draw a small X on the plate where you think the tip of the shadow will be.

5 Check the position of the shadow every hour and trace the outline of the shadow directly onto the plate. Write the number of the hour (1, 2, 3 . . .) on the plate at the end of the shadow. Continue doing this every hour until the sun sets.

6 If you choose, you can begin again in the same spot at sunrise and record the hours until noon to make a complete clock.

7 Write down your observations in your science journal. Why does the shadow seem to be moving? What object is actually moving?

TRY THIS: Research sundials online to see how other people have designed them. Can you find the largest one? How about the smallest? Oldest? How have sundials changed since ancient times?

COOL CONCEPT

The Greeks named the sun after their god of the sun, Helios. They believed Helios pulled the sun across the sky each day with his chariot.

HOW POWERFUL IS SUNLIGHT?

IDEAS FOR SUPPLIES
*dark-colored construction paper * various small toys or objects*

We know sunlight helps plants grow, evaporates water, and can burn our skin. We can even generate renewable energy from the sun using solar panels, wind turbines, and other technologies. What else can sunlight do? You need a sunny day to do this activity!

1 Put two pieces of paper directly in the sun at or around noon. Keep the other piece inside.

2 Place some toys on one of the pieces of paper in the sun and trace them with a pencil.

3 What do you think will happen to the paper? To the objects? Think about the heat and the light from the sun. Organize your predictions in your science journal using a chart such as the one below.

	Prediction	Observation After 45 Minutes
Paper in the sun		
Paper in the sun with toys		
Paper out of the sun		

4 After 45 minutes, compare the three pieces of construction paper. How are they different? How are they similar? What caused the differences? On a cloudy day, would it take longer to see any changes?

TRY THIS: Draw two pictures on two pieces of construction paper using ice cubes. Set one picture in the sun and the other inside for 30 minutes. What happens to the pictures? Why?

IDEAS FOR SUPPLIES
*drawing materials * 7-day weather forecast*

How is weather different from climate? Weather can be described as the day-to-day conditions. From a bright, sunny day to a snowy day, weather can change quickly. Climate, on the other hand, is made up of long-term weather patterns across many years. Let's explore some of the characteristics of weather.

1 Think of three characteristics of weather that might influence temperature, such as humidity, clouds, and wind. Read or watch the 7-day forecast from a few different sources.

2 Make your own predictions for the next seven days. Be sure to predict for the same hour of each day.

3 Collect data on the weather for one week at the same time of day for the same location. Use a data table like the one below to record your predictions and data.

Date	Prediction	Temperature	Characteristics of weather		

4 What did you learn about the weather? How did your predictions compare to your data? Were the 7-day forecasts correct? Why do forecasters often get the weather wrong?

MAKE AN APPLE BATTERY

How do we keep solar energy working at night? Batteries! We use batteries as a way of storing energy. Batteries create electricity from a chemical reaction. A piece of fruit, such as an apple, is an example of nature's battery. The sun's energy is stored in the fruit's sugars and starches. We can use those sugars and starches to create electricity. Start a scientific method worksheet in your science journal to organize, gather, and analyze your data. Practice using your multimeter with a working AA (1.5 volt) or 9-volt battery to ensure your circuit is properly wired.

starch: a type of **nutrient** found in certain foods, such as bread, potatoes, and rice.

nutrients: substances in food and soil that living things need to live and grow.

analyze: to study and examine.

WORDS2KNOW

1 Insert the copper and zinc nails into the apple, making sure they don't touch or go all the way through the fruit.

Handyman Multimeter

A handyman multimeter is a scientific instrument that measures volts. A volt is the unit used to measure the potential energy, sometimes called stored energy, between two spots in a circuit. The path of a circuit lets electricity flow when it is closed in a loop.

2 Measure the distance between the nails and record it in your science journal.

3 Connect the wire to both nails with alligator clips and check the multimeter. How many volts is your apple battery producing? Record your results.

4 What do you think will happen if you put the nails closer together or farther apart? Write your hypothesis in your journal and then move your nails to different distances and record the results. Does the electricity get stronger or weaker? Why?

TRY THIS: What will happen if the copper and zinc nails are inserted into the apple less or more deeply? What would happen if you change the size of the nails? Record your hypotheses and perform each test. Don't forget to record your results! You can also try using a lemon or potato for a battery. Do you think other fruits or vegetables will be better or worse than the apple?

43

BUILD YOUR OWN ANEMOMETER

IDEAS FOR SUPPLIES
*5 paper cups * paint * thin wooden dowels or chopsticks * empty water bottle*

Windmills convert the energy in wind to do other types of work. Harnessing wind power dates back to Greece in the first century! Here you are going to make an anemometer, which is a device that is used to measure wind speed.

1 Take four paper cups and punch a single hole halfway down the side of each cup. Paint one cup a color different from the others.

2 On the fifth cup, make four holes evenly spaced around the rim. The first and third holes should be slightly closer to the rim than the second and fourth holes. Carefully punch one hole in the center of the bottom of this cup.

3 Slide two of the dowels through the holes in the fifth cup to make an X. Make sure the first four cups are all on their sides facing the same direction. Connect each through the hole in its side to an end of each of the dowels. Secure each cup to its dowel with tape. Why should they all be facing the same direction?

4 Insert a dowel through the hole in the bottom of the fifth cup until it meets the X. Tape the X and the center dowel together.

5 Place the center dowel in an empty water bottle and let the center cup rest on top. Blow into one of the cups to test if your anemometer is working. Then take your anemometer outside to see if it works in the wind. Why did we make one cup different from the others?

6 Record how many rotations your anemometer makes in 30 seconds. What changes can you make to the windmill to make it spin faster? Record your ideas in your science journal.

TRY THIS: Design a different anemometer. Does it work better than the original anemometer? Why? How do you know if it works better?

COOL CONCEPT

There are two renewable energy solutions that are not powered by the sun. Geothermal energy comes from heat deep in the earth and tidal energy comes from the pull of the moon on the water in the oceans. We'll explore these energy sources in Chapter 6.

CHAPTER 3
BURPS, FARTS, AND OTHER GREENHOUSE GASES

Just as Spaceship Earth relies on a series of highly **interconnected** systems for survival, so do our bodies. A change in one system can upset the balance of the entire human body, or the entire world.

Do you ever fart or burp a lot after eating certain foods? During digestion, our bodies produce a special mix of **enzymes** and **acids** called digestive juices that live in our intestines along with billions of **bacteria**. Together, the digestive juices and bacteria break down foods so nutrients can be carried by our blood and used by our cells. While creating the energy our bodies need to walk, talk, grow, and survive, this process also releases gases.

? ESSENTIAL QUESTION

Why are the carbon cycle and water cycle important to the earth's climate? What happens when they get disrupted?

Humans can fart more than 20 times a day, releasing small amounts of nitrogen, carbon dioxide, and methane. The cause of the odor from a fart is sulfur in your diet. Sulfur is found naturally in some grains, fruits, vegetables, and meats. Garlic, broccoli, chicken, fish, and beef all contain sulfur.

equilibrium: to be in balance.

excess: more than the normal amount.

WORDS 2 KNOW

COOL CONCEPT

What happens when you eat lots of one kind of food, such as candy or cookies? You might not feel very well afterward. Your digestive system might be out of balance and you might burp and fart more.

The same thing can happen to the systems on Spaceship Earth. Many human activities, such as burning fossil fuels for energy, release greenhouse gases into the atmosphere. It's important that these gases are kept in a careful **equilibrium** because **excess** greenhouse gases unbalance the climate on Earth. The three most important greenhouse gases in our atmosphere are methane, water vapor, and carbon dioxide.

The sun is Earth's largest source of energy. Yet humans get 90 percent of all energy from burning fossil fuels.

Methane in the Mix

Our atmosphere is a mixture of many gases. Carbon is present in the atmosphere as carbon dioxide and methane. Methane is far less abundant than carbon dioxide. For every molecule of methane in the earth's atmosphere there are 235 molecules of carbon dioxide.

But methane is a more powerful heat-trapping gas than carbon dioxide. It absorbs 25 times more solar energy than carbon dioxide. Human activities release less methane than carbon dioxide, but it is important to know how this heat-trapping gas contributes to global warming.

Methane comes from a few different sources. One of those sources gives us steak and hamburgers. There are

more than 1.5 billion cows on the planet that release massive amounts of methane as they digest their food. Cows burp and fart just like humans, and they release methane when they fart. In fact, they are one of the world's largest producers of methane.

permafrost: in far northern areas, the ground underneath the top layer of soil that is permanently frozen.

WORDS 2 KNOW

COOL CONCEPT

Methane can also be found leaking from the ocean floor and frozen in the **permafrost** of Siberia. What will happen if that frozen ground thaws out? Where will the methane go?

Good Bugs

Termites also produce methane as they digest wood. Cows and termites rely on a **symbiotic** relationship with bacteria in their bodies to help them digest their food. Do humans need microorganisms to digest our food? Yes! There are more than 500 **species** of microorganisms inside the human digestive system. We can't live without them.

Another way methane is released into the atmosphere is through human use of fossil fuels. Natural gas and oil systems are the largest sources of methane **emissions** in the United States. We use natural gas to heat our homes and fuel our stoves. Methane is released into the atmosphere during the production, processing, storage, shipping, and use of natural gas.

The production, transportation, and storage of crude oil are also sources of methane emissions. We use oil for transportation and generation of electricity. Finally, as our trash **decomposes** in landfills, methane is released. Landfills are the third-largest source of methane emissions in the United States. As more and more people throw out more stuff, what happens to methane levels?

Remember, small changes in the amount of greenhouse gases can upset the balance in the atmosphere just as small changes in your diet can have an effect on how you feel.

symbiotic: the relationship between two different kinds of living things that depend on each other.

species: a group of living things that are closely related and look similar.

WORDS 2 KNOW

emission: something sent or given off, such as smoke, gas, heat, or light.

decompose: to rot or decay.

49

respiratory system: the parts of the body used to breathe.

regulate: to control something.

photosynthesis: the process in which plants use sunlight, water, and carbon dioxide to create energy.

evolve: to gradually develop through time and become more complex.

WORDS2KNOW

Carbon Dioxide in the Air

Take a deep breath and blow it back out. What's happening? Where is the air going? What parts of our body are doing the work? We breathe all day, every day, without thinking much about it. Your **respiratory system** keeps you alive by breathing in oxygen to create energy and breathing out carbon dioxide as a waste product. All animals have a respiratory system that breathes in oxygen and releases carbon dioxide.

Planet Earth has a respiratory system, too. The forests and oceans act as lungs to help **regulate** the balance of gases in our atmosphere. But there's a big difference. Plants absorb carbon dioxide while releasing oxygen. This process is known as **photosynthesis**.

Life on Earth has evolved to produce two perfectly interconnected systems. Plants breathe out what humans and animals need, and humans and animals breathe out what plants need.

Do ants breathe? Yes! Don't forget, insects are animals. They breathe in oxygen and breathe out carbon dioxide just like people.

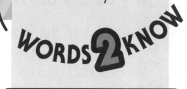

carbon cycle: the movement of carbon through the earth's ecosystems.

WORDS 2 KNOW

COOL CONCEPT

Go outside and look at the biggest tree you can find. Trees grow just as you do, with energy they gain from things they consume. That doesn't mean trees eat apples or cheddar cheese. Trees grow taller and wider by absorbing carbon dioxide from the air during photosynthesis.

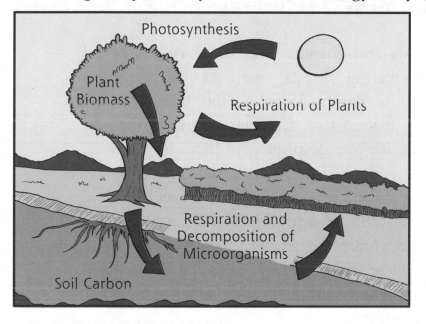

Photosynthesis

Plant Biomass

Respiration of Plants

Respiration and Decomposition of Microorganisms

Soil Carbon

That big tree outside your window contains thousands of pounds of carbon that it has absorbed right out of the air. A healthy tree can absorb up to 50 pounds of carbon dioxide from the atmosphere each year.

When a tree burns, all of its trapped carbon is released back into the atmosphere. The process of adding and subtracting carbon from the earth's atmosphere is called the **carbon cycle**. Just like methane, carbon dioxide needs to be balanced in the atmosphere. When there is too much carbon in one place, such as in the ocean or in the air, there are consequences for the climate.

See For Yourself

Explore the world of greenhouse gases with this live scenario tool. How is energy from the sun impacted by adding or subtracting carbon dioxide and nitrogen? What happens to the sunlight and the heat? What effect does nitrogen have on our climate?

boreal forest: a northern forest filled mostly with conifers, which are trees with needles that produce cones. Most conifers are evergreens that do not lose their leaves each year.

agriculture: growing crops and raising animals for food.

WORDS 2 KNOW

Scientists and citizens alike are very concerned about protecting forests, such as the Amazon rainforest in South America, the Cloud Forest in Costa Rica, and Canada's **boreal forests**. Yet, sadly, we are destroying millions of acres of forestland each year through human activity, such as cutting down trees for paper and fuel and clearing the land for **agriculture**. This means our planet's lungs are getting smaller while at the same time we are releasing more and more carbon dioxide into the atmosphere.

One way an individual citizen can take positive action to help the climate is to plant a tree. During the course of a tree's life it can absorb thousands of pounds of carbon dioxide right out of the air. More strategies for protecting our climate can be found in Chapter 6.

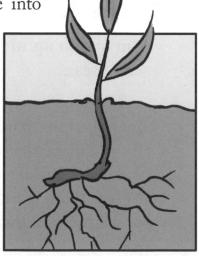

Carbon Dioxide in the Water

dissolve: when molecules of one substance get mixed into the molecules of another substance.

Oceans are another part of the earth's respiratory system. They play an extremely important role in absorbing carbon dioxide from our atmosphere.

Anywhere that air touches the surface of water, a few molecules of carbon dioxide are able to **dissolve** in the water. Since 70 percent of the earth's surface is covered with water, that leads to 1.7 gigatons of carbon dioxide absorption. That's the same as the weight of 85,000,000 blue whales!

What happens to the carbon dioxide absorbed by the ocean? Many ocean organisms use that carbon dioxide to create their shells. Have you ever walked down the beach and collected shells? Those are formed from carbon!

sedimentary layer: a layer of rock formed from the compression of sediments, the remains of plants and animals, or from the evaporation of seawater.

limestone: a kind of rock that forms from the skeletons and shells of sea creatures.

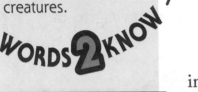

Carbon dioxide is also absorbed by tiny organisms called phytoplankton. Phytoplankton are plants called marine algae found floating on the surface of the ocean. As with all plants, they breathe in carbon dioxide and release oxygen. Phytoplankton are so abundant in the ocean that they can be seen from space!

Phytoplankton are responsible for producing 50 percent of the oxygen we breathe.

Carbon dioxide that is not used by life forms in the ocean sinks slowly to the bottom, where it accumulates in **sedimentary layers**. After millions of years, this large accumulation of carbon on the ocean floor turns into rock known as **limestone**. Limestone is found all over the planet.

Water Everywhere

The water cycle plays an important role in regulating the earth's temperature. Water is in continuous movement above and below the surface of the earth. Because of the water cycle, the water you drink today is the same water the dinosaurs swam in and drank more than 65 million years ago.

The water cycle transports the sun's energy from one place to another and changes its state between liquid, solid, and gas, depending on where the water is and how hot or cold it is. Oceans, lakes, and drinking cups contain liquid water. Ice trays and glaciers contain solid water. The atmosphere contains water vapor, which makes clouds, rain, and snow.

The most famous limestone cliffs in the world are in Dover, England, called the White Cliffs of Dover. These cliffs are evidence of the massive amounts of carbon that our oceans absorb.

sea level: the level of the surface of the sea.

WORDS **2** KNOW

COOL CONCEPT

When liquid water evaporates to form water vapor, it absorbs heat. This process helps keep the earth's surface the right temperature for life. When water vapor condenses in the atmosphere to form precipitation, it releases heat. The releasing of this heat also helps to regulate temperature. Water vapor in the earth's atmosphere absorbs and reflects much of the sun's energy. That is why water vapor is also considered a greenhouse gas.

The water cycle is essential for life on Earth.

It might sound strange that water helps to both heat and cool the earth, but as long as the system stays balanced, the earth stays the right temperature. Small changes in our climate can have significant impacts on the water cycle. This means that some places might be affected by drought. Coastal areas see rising **sea levels**. These consequences affect our ability to produce food and energy.

Tracing the Movement of Water

Explore more of the interactions within the water cycle. This website allows you to investigate all the parts of the water cycle. Click on any part in the cycle to learn more.

Don't Sweat It!

Do you get sweaty when you exercise? That's your body's way of regulating its temperature. When the sweat on your skin evaporates, it absorbs heat, just like water absorbs heat when it evaporates into the atmosphere. Your body cools off, just like the earth cools off, through evaporation.

What happens when the systems get out of balance? In the next chapter we will explore changes in our climate. By understanding our ancient climates we can begin to see how human activities and the burning of fossil fuels are disrupting our atmosphere's balance.

Life on Earth depends on the balance of the interconnected systems of the water cycle and the carbon cycle.

? **ESSENTIAL QUESTION**

Now it's time to consider and discuss the Essential Question: Why are the carbon cycle and water cycle important to the earth's climate? What happens when they get disrupted?

MEASURE THE MOISTURE IN THE AIR

IDEAS FOR SUPPLIES
jar with a lid

What does your skin feel like on a hot, sticky day? Moist and wet? That's because there is moisture in the air. You can find evidence of moisture in the air with this experiment.

1 Start a scientific method worksheet. What will happen to a jar of air when you heat it up or cool it down? Record your hypothesis. What will this tell you about the moisture in the air?

2 Put the lid on your jar and place it in a shady spot outside for about 10 minutes. Observe what happens to the air inside the jar during this time and record what you notice.

3 Freeze your jar for 90 minutes, then set it on a table. It will be really cold! What do you see? What happened to the air inside the jar? What does this tell you about the amount of moisture? Record your observations in your science journal. Compare your results to your predictions.

TRY THIS: Repeat this experiment in different locations with different temperatures. Try different types of containers. What happens?

COOL CONCEPT

The amount of water vapor in the air varies depending on the climate on the ground. Where do you think you'll find the most water vapor in the air? The least?

COOL DOWN WITH EVAPORATION

IDEAS FOR SUPPLIES
rubbing alcohol ✳ *eye dropper* ✳ *clock or timer*

When water evaporates, it uses energy to transform from a liquid into a gas. This use of energy leaves the area cooler. Test the process of evaporation with rubbing alcohol, a liquid that evaporates quickly.

Caution: While rubbing alcohol is safe to put on your skin, it is toxic to drink. Be sure to keep it away from your eyes. Ask an adult to help you handle the rubbing alcohol.

1 Start a scientific method worksheet in your journal. What will happen to your skin as the rubbing alcohol evaporates? Record your hypothesis.

2 Place 5 to 10 drops of rubbing alcohol on the back of your hand. Start your timer. Can you feel the rubbing alcohol evaporating? What does it feel like?

3 Wait for the drops to evaporate. How long does it take? Does your skin feel different after the liquid evaporates? Record your observations in your science journal.

TRY THIS: Which evaporates faster, rubbing alcohol or water? Try the experiment again using water on your hand instead of rubbing alcohol. Time how long it takes for the water to evaporate. Is it faster or slower than rubbing alcohol? Does your skin feel cooler or warmer after the water evaporates?

MAKE YOUR OWN ICE

IDEAS FOR SUPPLIES
*empty ice cube tray * stove * freezer * 2 clear cups*

Have you ever noticed that water from different places can taste different? This is because different substances can dissolve in water and change the taste. Air can also dissolve into water. When water freezes, air bubbles get trapped in the ice. But what happens when you boil water before you freeze it? Find out by forming ice from two types of water.

Caution: Ask an adult to help you boil the water for this experiment.

1 Start a scientific method worksheet in your science journal. Will ice made from different types of water be different in any way?

2 Label one side of your ice cube tray "boiled water" and the other side "tap water."

3 Have an adult help you boil some water. Fill half the ice cube tray with regular tap water and the other half with the boiled water. Freeze the ice cube tray for three hours.

4 Collect the tap water ice in one glass and the boiled water ice in another glass. What's different about them? Record your observations.

5 Fill each glass with water. Do they smell different? Do they taste different?

THINK ABOUT IT: Scientists can learn about changes in the earth's atmosphere by drilling into glaciers. Air bubbles trapped in the ice give clues about the atmosphere during different periods of time. Did you observe air bubbles in your ice?

EXPERIMENT WITH DRY ICE

IDEAS FOR SUPPLIES
*tongs * gloves * safety goggles * dry ice * dish soap * food coloring*

The North and South Poles of Mars have ice caps just as the poles of Earth have ice caps. The ice on Mars, however, is much different. On Earth, polar ice is made of frozen water. On Mars, polar ice is made of frozen carbon dioxide. To learn about carbon dioxide as both a solid and a gas, experiment with dry ice. Like the polar ice on Mars, dry ice is made from frozen carbon dioxide.

Caution: Have an adult work with you when you experiment with dry ice. Dry ice can cause frostbite if you touch it with your skin. Wear safety goggles and rubber gloves and use tongs to move dry ice. You can purchase dry ice at most grocery stores, although you may have to call in advance. Buy the dry ice the day you plan to use it and carry it in an open bucket, not an airtight container. Open the windows while in the car to keep fresh oxygen in the air. The clouds that form when working with dry ice are safe for you to touch and feel.

LET'S DO SOME SCIENCE

1 Start a scientific method worksheet in your science journal. What can you learn about carbon dioxide from experimenting with dry ice? Make your prediction.

2 Use tongs and wear gloves to place a piece of dry ice on a plate. Place a piece of regular ice on a different plate. Leave the ice for one hour. What happens? Why do you think frozen carbon dioxide is called dry ice? Record your observations.

3 While you are waiting for the hour to pass, fill a glass halfway with warm water. Use the tongs and gloves to place a piece of dry ice in the glass. What happens? Add more warm water to the glass after a couple of minutes and observe the results.

4 Add a squirt of liquid dish soap to the warm water. How does this change the behavior of the dry ice?

Carefully.

5 Add food coloring to the glass of water. What happens to the gas? Record your observations in your science journal.

GIANTS OF SCIENCE

Joseph Black and Joseph Priestley

In 1754, Joseph Black (1728–1799) discovered the existence of carbon dioxide. Twenty years later, another scientist, named Joseph Priestley (1733–1804), discovered oxygen. Without these two, we'd still believe that air is one single substance. Black also discovered that carbon dioxide is denser than air and can put out fire. Today, we use carbon dioxide in fire extinguishers.

CHAPTER 4
TIME-TRAVELING SCIENTISTS

coral reef: an underwater ecosystem made by coral.

tree rings: layers of wood inside a tree added each year as it grows.

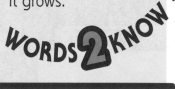

The climate today is very different from the climate the dinosaurs experienced. We know that the earth's climate is constantly changing, but what's the best way to find clues about our planet's past climate? By traveling back in time!

Scientists do this in many ways. They examine fossils to see what lived at different times in the past. They study gases trapped in ice to learn about ancient atmospheres. They read the clues written in **coral reefs**, muddy ocean floors, and **tree rings** to understand climate at different points in time.

? ESSENTIAL QUESTION

Why is it important to study the climate of the past? How does understanding the past help us understand the present?

Scientists gather data about ancient environments in order to better understand today's climate. Let's begin by going back in time to when most of the earth was covered in ice.

Icy Times

Glaciers once covered much more of the earth than they do today. While glaciers can still be found around the globe in the oceans and on land, there are far

fewer and those that remain are smaller. The oldest glaciers are in Antarctica and Greenland. **Glaciologists** study glaciers to learn about the earth's changing climate.

The frozen portion of the earth is called the cryosphere.

Glaciers may seem very still, but they are always moving. As they move, glaciers deposit rocks and leave scrapes on the surface of the earth. These scrapes and rock piles help scientists understand in what direction and how far the glaciers moved. Scientists have mapped glacial movement around the globe to better understand climate change. Because of our changing climate, most glaciers are shrinking.

Have you ever been to Central Park in New York City? You can see the glacial scrapes, called striations, on rocks there. Long Island, New York, was formed by a giant glacier thousands of years ago. As the glacier melted, it left behind a pile of rocks that is now Long Island. Can you find Glacier National Park on a map?

Scientists drill down into glaciers and collect **ice cores** to study the earth's ancient atmosphere. They analyze gas bubbles in the ice cores to measure the amount of greenhouse gases that were present in the atmosphere in the past, as far back as 800,000 years.

The ice core data shows that during the last 800,000 years, the amount of carbon dioxide in the atmosphere remained constant, until around the 1850s. Since then, carbon dioxide levels have jumped nearly 45 percent, from 250 parts per million (ppm) to more than 400 ppm.

GIANTS OF SCIENCE

Richard Alley

Glaciologist Richard Alley (1957–present) has drilled 2 miles down into Greenland's glaciers! His team works in below-freezing temperatures to pull up ice cores from 110,000 years ago. Can you imagine a glacier that is 2 miles thick? Picture 34 Statues of Liberty stacked on top of each other. The island country of Greenland is covered in glaciers. What happens if Greenland's glaciers all melt into the sea?

Glaciers can be found in Montana, Washington, Alaska, and even California! In 1850, Glacier National Park in Montana had 150 glaciers. Today, due to climate change, the park has 25 active glaciers. Scientists predict that by 2020, that number could be zero.

diverse: a large variety.

WORDS 2 KNOW

COOL CONCEPT

Glaciers tell us there are more greenhouse gases in the atmosphere now than at any time during the past 800,000 years. This imbalance of greenhouse gases is causing global warming, which is melting glaciers around the globe.

As the glaciers melt, they add large amounts of water to the oceans, making the sea level rise—so far by more than 6 inches. Melting glaciers are a problem for anyone who lives near a coastline, which is more than half of the earth's inhabitants. Glaciologist Richard Alley predicts that up to 70 percent of all glaciers could melt by 2100.

Coral Reefs

Coral reefs are one of the most **diverse** and oldest ecosystems on the planet. Coral reefs are made from tiny organisms called corals, which settle on rocks and form hard shells of calcium. Millions of individual corals, called polyps, settle in large groups. With time, their small, hard shells accumulate, making huge structures that are home to colorful algae, plankton, and fish. Called the rainforests of the ocean, coral reefs are found in shallow, warm waters.

Many organisms can't survive if the ocean temperature increases or decreases by even a few degrees.

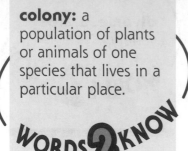

colony: a population of plants or animals of one species that lives in a particular place.

WORDS 2 KNOW

The ocean is the largest unexplored place on Earth—less than 5 percent of it has been explored.

Corals are among the oldest known living marine organisms. Scientists have found 4,000-year-old coral **colonies** in Australia. Their extremely long life spans make coral reefs a wonderful place to study changes in climate. Scientists study coral reefs in a variety of ways—through observation, collecting samples, and chemical analysis.

When observing corals, scientists look for changes in color and size as indicators of their health. Corals get their color from sunlight absorbed by algae that live in their tissues. These algae give coral reefs their beautiful colors. When corals lose that color, scientists know they're unhealthy.

Coral reefs are also one of the slowest-growing organisms on Earth, growing 2 to 3 centimeters a year. That's slower than your fingernails! The Great Barrier Reef is 1,553 miles long and the Red Sea Coral Reef is 1,180 miles long. Scientists estimate that it took these two reefs more than 100,000 years to grow to their current sizes.

COOL CONCEPT

How fast do you grow? Think about how tall you were when you were born and how tall you are now. Find your average growth by taking your current height in inches and dividing it by your age.

Close up of coral bands.

You can see the largest coral reef from outer space! The Australian Great Barrier Reef stretches more than 1,500 miles.

Scientists also take samples of living and dead corals. They compare **coral band** thickness with their data on carbon dioxide in the atmosphere. Thinner coral layers indicate slower growth. Remember the oceans absorb massive amounts of carbon dioxide just as our forests do. Increases in carbon dioxide in the atmosphere lead to increases in carbon dioxide absorption by the ocean and **ocean acidification**. The coral bands are thinner because ocean acidification causes corals to grow more slowly.

Global warming is also causing changes to ocean temperature and sea level. Warming water temperatures and increased acidity harm the algae in coral reefs, causing them to lose color or die. This is called **coral bleaching** because the coral turns white.

coral band: a layer added each year to coral reefs.

ocean acidification: when oceans absorb too much carbon dioxide and become more acidic.

coral bleaching: a sign of poor health in coral that happens when algae in the coral die or lose their color.

WORDS 2 KNOW

PS Explore the Deep

Citizens and scientists contribute to our knowledge by taking photos of coral reef systems all around the world. These photos allow observations of size and color of coral reefs. Explore these underwater photos.

microfossil: a tiny fossil that can be seen only with a microscope.

WORDS 2 KNOW

Coral bleaching can stunt the growth of coral, leave them exposed to disease, and even kill them. Nearly 60 percent of coral reefs around the world are at risk of coral bleaching. Additionally, rising sea levels decrease the amount of sunlight reaching corals, which is another factor that impacts their growth. Studying coral growth helps scientists understand how changing conditions in the atmosphere are changing conditions in the ocean.

Mud Pies From the Deep Sea

On a hot summer's day, it's fun to wade in the ocean and feel squishy, cool mud between your toes. If you pull up a handful of that mud, you might find small rocks and pieces of seashells. There are also tiny shells in the mud that you can't see. These are called **microfossils**.

Using state-of-the-art equipment, scientists drill the ocean floor much like glaciologists drill into glaciers. They collect mud cores to study. Scientists pay extra-close attention to the microfossils at each layer in the cores. Looking at the tiny shells found at different depths tells us about the earth's changing climate.

COOL CONCEPT

The *JOIDES Resolution* has collected more than 100 miles of mud core for the Ocean Drilling Program. The deepest hole drilled was more than a mile into the ocean floor. Learn more here.

The chemistry of shells from tiny microscopic animals, called foraminifera, radiolarians, and diatoms, gives us clues about ocean temperatures, wind patterns, and sea levels.

Diatoms are a type of algae that are early indicators of the impact of climate change, including changes in sea level. As the temperature of water changes, so does the population. Diatoms can be found in both deep-water and shallow-water areas. Since the 1850s, there has been dramatic changes in diatom and radiolarian communities found in Arctic waters.

How far into the past can we travel with mud? It all depends on the type of water. In fresh water, every 3 feet of mud is equal to a thousand years! Next time you walk into a lake, remember you could dig down and touch mud that could be a thousand years old. Saltwater oceans and seas accumulate layers of mud more slowly. In the deep ocean, a half inch of mud equals a thousand years.

How long a line would equal 10,000 years of deep ocean mud?

Diversity of Radiolarian Design

Check out these amazing photographs of radiolarians. They have an incredible diversity of design.

You can also watch this video of lake ecologist Jasmine Saros and her University of Maine team studying radiolarians in southwestern Greenland.

Rings of Time

Trees can live to be more than 5,000 years old. In California, a giant Sequoia tree named the President is 3,200 years old! As a tree grows older, it adds a new layer of wood each year, called a tree ring. Tree rings show evidence of changes in the environment just as ice and mud do. Scientists study tree rings to estimate temperatures on Earth before climate measurements were recorded. This study of tree rings is called dendrochronology.

Dendron = tree, chronos = time, and logos = the study of

Dendrochronologists examine trees and stumps or they drill into a tree and pull out a core, just as glaciologists take cores from glaciers. First, scientists count the tree rings to determine its age. Then they measure the thickness of the rings, which provides information about the precipitation and temperature that occurred during that year. For example, a wet season causes thicker tree rings and a dry season causes thinner tree rings. Changes in temperature can also affect the thickness of a tree ring.

Tree Rings

Liz Smith is a tree historian who helps us understand climate by studying tree rings. Tree rings tell us how old a tree is and give us clues about its environment as it grew. Check out this video to explore the data we are able to gather from tree rings.

Walking With Dinosaurs

Paleontologists can reconstruct the earth's climate history from millions and even billions of years ago by looking at the **fossil record**. Through fossils, scientists know that some of the coldest places on Earth were once tropical rainforests. For example, fossil ferns from the **Mesozoic Era** could not have lived in freezing temperatures. This means that there were probably no glaciers during the time of the dinosaurs.

Geologists can even travel back more than 2 billion years to the era before the first animals lived. This was when there was almost no oxygen in the earth's atmosphere.

paleontologist: a scientist who studies fossils.

fossil record: a record of information of the past that a collection of fossils can provide.

Mesozoic Era: a period of time from about 252 to 66 million years ago, when dinosaurs roamed the earth.

geologist: a scientist who studies the history, structure, and origin of the earth.

WORDS 2 KNOW

Geologists study fossils of stromalites, one of the oldest organisms in the earth's history. Stromalites are a type of blue-green algae that uses photosynthesis to make its own food. They are formed by the growth of layer upon layer of cyanobacteria, a type of bacteria that still exists in parts of Australia and Mexico.

Geologists have found fossils of stromalites all over the globe from 2 billion years ago. That is when, almost overnight, the amount of oxygen in our atmosphere increased because stromalites started releasing oxygen into the air, just as trees do now!

Industrial Revolution: a period of time beginning in the late 1700s when people started using machines to make things in large factories.

WORDS 2 KNOW

In 2011, scientists found 200-million-year-old dinosaur fossils known to be warm weather animals about 6,600 feet up the icy St. Kirkpatrick mountain in Antarctica. This discovery helped scientists understand that Antarctica was once a lot warmer.

COOL CONCEPT

Glaciers, coral reefs, mud, and trees provide lots of information about the earth's climate. They show that while climate has always gone through changes, today climate change is happening much, much more quickly than it ever has before. Humans have released large amounts of greenhouse gases into the atmosphere from burning fossil fuels since the beginning of the **Industrial Revolution**. Scientists have found evidence that this is responsible for global warming and climate change. In less than 150 years, the concentrations of carbon dioxide in the atmosphere have increased 45 percent. Remember what happens with too much carbon dioxide in the atmosphere?

? ESSENTIAL QUESTION

Now it's time to consider and discuss the Essential Question: Why is it important to study the climate of the past? How does understanding the past help us understand the present?

Heating Up

One way scientists know that the climate is changing is by recording temperatures across a long period of time. Watch this fast-paced animation that shows the average temperature increases between 1950 and 2013. Do you think the video shows that the climate is changing?

FOSSIL COLLECTION

IDEAS FOR SUPPLIES

small objects such as shells, rocks, plastic toys, or leaves ∗ ½ cup flour ∗ ½ cup used coffee grounds ∗ ¼ cup salt ∗ ¼ cup sand ∗ magnifying glass

Fossils are the remains or impressions of plants or animals that lived long ago, preserved in rock. They provide clues about ancient life. You can create your own fossils of objects you have collected. Make your own fossil dough or purchase Plaster of Paris.

1 Mix all the dry ingredients together. Make a thick dough by adding a little water. You want a dough that isn't crumbly or too sticky.

2 On a flat surface, knead the dough and press it into a slab a few centimeters thick.

3 Push your objects into the dough to leave impressions. Remove the objects and let the dough dry for a few days.

4 Closely examine your impressions with a magnifying glass. What kinds of details can you observe? What do your fossils tell you about the objects that made them? Record your observations in your science journal.

Out of the Earth

NASA currently has more than 20 satellites orbiting Earth to study the oceans, forests, land, ice, and atmosphere. NASA satellites *GRACE* and *ICES* show rapid changes in the earth's great ice sheets. The *Jason-1* satellite records the sea levels rising at an increasing rate. Check out what kinds of data are collected from other NASA satellites.

SOIL SCIENTIST

IDEAS FOR SUPPLIES
clear jar with lid ✳ soil from 3 different locations ✳ timer

Soil can be found in many locations, from your back yard or the bottom of a river to the bottom of the ocean. It is made up of a mixture of sand, silt, organic material, and clay and comes in all shapes, colors, and thicknesses. In this experiment, you will explore the mixture of things found in soil, investigate the differences between soils from different areas, and look for clues about the surrounding environment.

1 Fill a clean, clear jar or bottle about a third of the way up with one kind of soil. What does the soil look like? Record your observations in your science journal.

2 Pour water into the jar until it's almost full. Do you notice any bubbles? What happens to the soil?

3 Put the top back on the jar or bottle and shake it vigorously for 20 seconds. How long do you think it will take before the soil settles? Record your hypothesis in your journal.

4 Time how long it takes for the water to turn clear. Keep in mind that some soils will take days to settle and for the water to turn clear. Record your observations in a chart such as the one on the next page.

Sample #	Time for soil to settle and water to clear	Do layers form? Describe them	Draw what you see
1			
2			
3			

5 Repeat with other soil samples. Try to find soil from unique locations. Why do you think it takes so long for the water to become completely clear? What kind of soil settles the quickest? The slowest? What does this mean for rivers, ponds, and oceans?

TRY THIS: Next time you are at the beach or lake, bring jars with you to reproduce this experiment. Record your results, and compare them with previous experiments.

GIANTS OF SCIENCE

PS

Benjamin Franklin

Americans have been studying climate since before we were even a country. Founding Father Benjamin Franklin (1706–1790) spent many hours studying the ocean and atmosphere. His recordings were published in a book called *Poor Richard's Almanack*. An almanac provides a record of weather, astronomy, and seasons through time and makes predictions for the coming year. Almanacs are still used today by farmers around the world. You can read a page of *Poor Richard's Almanack*, published in 1753.

OCEAN ACIDIFICATION

IDEAS FOR SUPPLIES
small cups ✳ *various liquid substances to test (see chart on the next page)* ✳
litmus paper *(found at hardware stores and aquarium supply stores)*

Our oceans are becoming more acidic. The pH of a liquid is measured on a scale of 0 to 14 and it tells us if a liquid is acidic. A pH of less than 7 is acidic. A pH of greater than 7 is basic. Pure water has a pH of 7. The farther a liquid's pH is from the number 7, the more acidic or basic it is. The most acidic liquid in the world has a pH of 0. Most organisms that live in the water need a pH range between 6 to 8.

1 Start a scientific method worksheet in your science journal. Create a chart like the one on the following page to record your observations.

2 Make a prediction about what the pH of common household substances will be. Remember, a pH of less than 7 is an acid, more than 7 is a base. Use your chart to record your predictions.

3 Pour small amounts of each substance into the cups. Dip your litmus paper into each cup and record the results for each substance.

litmus paper: a special paper used to test whether a substance is an acid or base.

WORDS 2 KNOW

4 Compare the results to your prediction.

Substance	Your Prediction	pH (litmus paper)
distilled water		
tap water		
rain water		
soda water		
vinegar		
lemon juice		
cola		
milk		
baking soda (mix with distilled water)		
aspirin (crush one pill and mix with 4 teaspoons of distilled water)		
shampoo		
soap		

TRY THIS: Make a new data table and make predictions of what the pHs will be when you mix substances together. Only use the items from this list. Do not use strong acids or bases, because they are dangerous. **Do not use bleach.**

CORE SAMPLING

Scientists use core sampling to study what lies beneath the surface. They take core samples of ice, coral, trees, mud, and rock. In this lab you will extract and examine core samples from food.

1 With a friend or parent, prepare vanilla cupcakes according to the package directions—only with a twist. Mix up the batter and divide it between three or more bowls. Use food coloring to make a different color of batter in each of the bowls.

2 Layer the batter of different colors in the muffin cups. If possible, layer in different thicknesses, varying the order and thicknesses in each cupcake. Bake the cupcakes according to the instructions.

3 While you wait, write down in your journal your predictions for what your core samples will look like. Which colors will be thicker and which will be thinner?

4 Once your cupcakes are out of the oven and cool, push a clear plastic straw into a cupcake. Rotate the straw through the cupcake as you push down. This will help you pull out the core sample.

Shrinking Glaciers

Scientists have tracked the size of glaciers for several decades. You can see photographs of glaciers now compared to a long time ago. Glaciers are shrinking all around the globe, from the Alps to Africa. Do they look different? What do you think they'll look like in another 20 years?

5 What colors are in your core sample? Was it hard to pull out your core? Make a drawing of what your sample actually looks like. Take a sample from each cupcake and observe the differences.

TRY THIS: Are there other foods that you can take core samples from? Do you need to use a different tool or technique? What kinds of problems do you encounter when taking a core sample? Think about how hard it might be to pull a core from the ice. What instruments might scientists need to use? How do scientists preserve ice cores to keep them from melting?

COOL CONCEPT

Did you know there is a kind of weather in space? Space weather happens when a solar storm from the sun travels through space. Energy released from solar storms can harm satellites and even disrupt the electricity in your home.

CHAPTER 5
MOTHER EARTH HAS A FEVER

Have you ever had a fever? What did it feel like? Your parents probably took your temperature and gave you medicine. Maybe they took you to the doctor.

Scientists have been taking the earth's temperature for more than 100 years. Like parents and doctors, scientists have used this temperature data to analyze and make **conclusions** about the health of our earth.

Their conclusion is that the earth has a fever. We call this fever global warming. The earth's rising temperature has been observed and recorded all around the globe, from deserts to glaciers, from mountaintops to ocean waters.

? ESSENTIAL QUESTION

How has human activity affected the earth's climate? How do we know?

How did the earth get a fever?
Mostly because of humans and human activities.

Earth's Fever

For the past 351 months, almost 30 years, global temperatures have been above the twentieth-century average. The fossil record, ice, coral reefs, mud, and tree rings all provide information about our past climate, which we can compare to our current climate.

We have evidence that human activities are impacting our climate at an alarming rate. Ninety-seven percent of **climatologists** agree that human activity is the driving force behind global warming. Scientific organizations around the world have issued public statements supporting this conclusion. In addition, governments around the world have issued similar supporting statements.

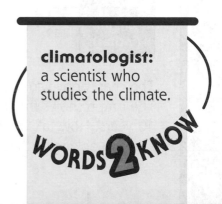

climatologist: a scientist who studies the climate.

WORDS 2 KNOW

PS

Fever Map

One of the easiest ways to check temperature changes through history and today is to read thermometers. Climatologists have used thermometers and weather stations in many places, such as Antarctica, Hawaii, and the North Pole to get temperatures since the 1880s. To display the increase in global temperatures, NASA uses a heat map. A heat map uses colors from blue to red to represent changes in temperature. What does the color red indicate?

You can also study heat maps and graphs of the United States from the Environmental Protection Agency. What do the graphs tell you?

Graphs

You'll find lots of graphs in this chapter. Reading and understanding graphs is an important part of being a scientist. It's a crucial step in analyzing a problem and looking for solutions. A graph is a picture of the data that makes it easier for a scientist to understand.

Age (years)	Born	1	2	3	4	5	6	7	8	9	10
Height (inches)	19	26	31	34	38	41	45	50	52	56	60

The chart above contains the data of a child's height compared to his or her age. The graph shows that data in a way that makes it easy to see the child's growth across 10 years. How tall was the child at age 9? How many inches did he or she grow since age 3? Looking at the graph, what do you notice about the child's growth?

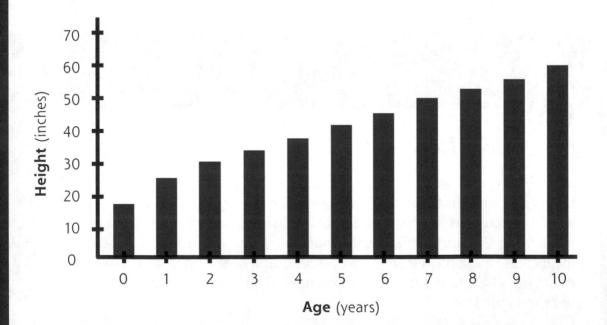

As the world's population grows, the demand for energy increases. Burning more and more fossil fuels to power our lives creates the earth's fever. Do you use a computer, phone, tablet, or television? Just think about our demand for all of this modern technology. These devices require energy. It takes energy to make electronic devices

and it takes energy to run them. Burning fossil fuels produces this energy, but it also releases greenhouses gases into the atmosphere. These greenhouse gases cause our earth to heat up.

This diagram of the earth shows where temperatures are warmer or colder than average. How much red do you see? How much blue?

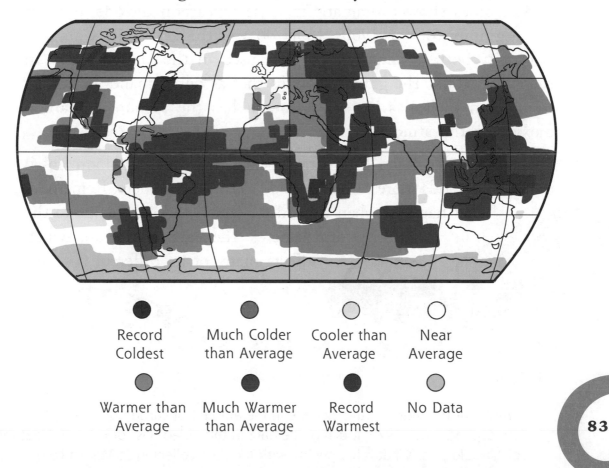

Now let's look at a graph that shows carbon dioxide levels in both air samples and ice cores. What do you think we'll find?

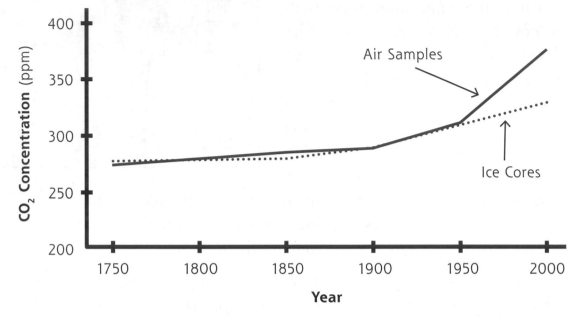

Both lines show a dramatic increase in carbon dioxide levels at the beginning of the 1900s. Why do you think that is? Cars and electricity both became more widely used in the United States in the early 1900s. The graphs show us that as our demand for energy from fossil fuels has increased, so too has the amount of carbon dioxide in the atmosphere.

Our increased need for energy means that we burn more fossil fuels, which adds more carbon dioxide to the atmosphere. Remember what happens when we add too much carbon dioxide to the atmosphere? The earth heats up, which affects many of its different systems.

COOL CONCEPT

Check out this video of the increase in the amount of carbon dioxide in the atmosphere since 1979. Much of the data in this video has come from the studies of glaciologists. What is happening with the data collected at Mauna Loa?

GIANTS OF SCIENCE

Warren Washington

Warren Washington (1936–present) holds a PhD in **meteorology** and is a leading expert in climate research. Using computer models, he has identified patterns and made predictions about greenhouse gases and temperature for the future. His computer models help identify relationships between activities such as burning fossil fuels and climate change.

Dinner!

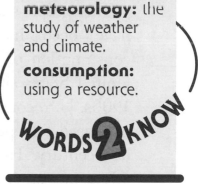

meteorology: the study of weather and climate.

consumption: using a resource.

WORDS 2 KNOW

Meat has more of an impact on the environment than any other food. As we learned in the previous chapter, methane contributes to global warming. The leading human activities releasing methane are drilling and mining for fossil fuels. The second-leading cause of methane is the large-scale production of cows, pigs, and chickens. Why are we growing and eating all these animals? Because we like meat! But that **consumption** of meat is impacting our climate.

Think about a hamburger. How much energy and resources did it take to get that hamburger on your plate? The sun grew the grass that the cow ate. Water fed that grass and the cow. Fuel was used to transport the meat from the farm to the meat packing plant to your grocery store, and then from the grocery store to your home. That is one long journey for a hamburger.

GROUND BEEF $2.99 per lb

The environmental costs of eating meat are significant. If you have a farm, you can use the land to grow vegetables that we eat directly or you can grow crops to be fed to animals. But you need to feed cattle 20 pounds of crops to create one pound of meat.

It takes a lot more energy to produce a pound of meat than it does to produce a pound of vegetables.

Animals raised as meat are environmentally troublesome for other reasons. When we concentrate lots of animals in a small area, we also concentrate their waste products, which can pollute the water and air.

This graph shows that we have been increasing our consumption of meat in the United States since the early 1900s. U.S. consumption has increased 500 percent in the last century. How does this affect our environment?

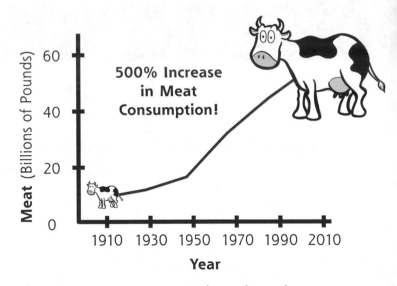

When looking at this data, it's important to remember that the human population was 1 billion people in 1800. Since then the human population has risen to 7 billion. Seven billion people need energy every day to cook their food, fuel their cars, build and light their homes, power factories, and recharge their electronics.

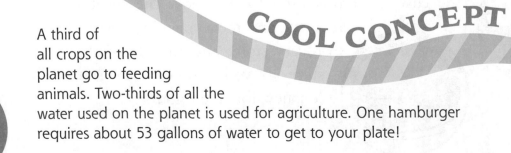

COOL CONCEPT

A third of all crops on the planet go to feeding animals. Two-thirds of all the water used on the planet is used for agriculture. One hamburger requires about 53 gallons of water to get to your plate!

The world population releases about 2 million pounds of carbon dioxide into the air every second. There are 86,400 seconds in a single day, so humans release 172 billion pounds of carbon dioxide into the atmosphere every day. All this excess carbon dioxide is what drives the changes in our climate.

One yellow school bus weighs 10,000 pounds. Americans release the weight of more than 700,000 school buses of carbon dioxide into our atmosphere from transportation—every day.

What Is Progress?

Not so long ago, the United States generated most of its electricity from renewable resources. For thousands of years, the human race relied on the energy from renewable sources for all of its cooking, heating, and lighting needs. More than 2,000 years ago we discovered how to harness wind and water to help us do our work. Windmills and watermills use the movement of air or water to power simple machines. When and why did humankind become so dependent on nonrenewable fossil fuels?

Have you ever been on a camping trip? If you don't bring a portable stove, how do you cook your food? For thousands of years, humans used fire for heat, light, and cooking. But a growing population in the United States used so much wood from forests to power their lives that the result was massive **deforestation**.

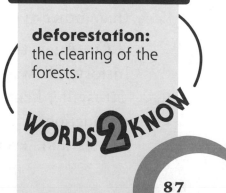

deforestation: the clearing of the forests.

WORDS2KNOW

Shifting Energy Sources

Since the United States was founded in 1776, our use of energy has been increasing. Read this article and study the graph about energy consumption patterns in the United States during the past 230 years. Notice our dependence on fossil fuels, including coal, natural gas, and petroleum. How did our energy use of these fuels change in the late 1800s?

During the first half of the 1800s, coal was burned to boil water, which created steam power for trains and boats. Coal became the main energy resource for transportation. In the 1880s, coal was first used to generate electricity for homes and factories. Today, coal is the largest source of electricity in the United States and around the world.

Around the same time we began using coal to power our trains and boats, we were using a massive amount of whale oil to light our homes. Whale oil became popular in the 1700s because it burned brighter and had less of a stinky odor than other types of oils.

On August 27, 1859, for the first time in human history, oil was tapped at its source in a field in Titusville, Pennsylvania. This led to the large-scale production and use of oil to heat and light our homes and, eventually, to power our cars.

Using oil as an energy source allowed for rapid **industrialization**. Oil powered the twentieth century and created the modern world as we know it. Just as the discovery of coal saved the forests, the discovery of oil saved the whale.

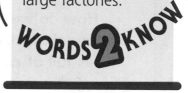

industrialization: when there is a lot of manufacturing, with products made by machines in large factories.

WORDS2KNOW

The history of our country is one of progress and energy transitions. We have changed how we power our lives through time, from renewables (wood, water, and wind), to fossil fuels (coal, natural gas, and petroleum). Our energy choices shape our society, climate, and our future. By understanding our energy use, we can answer questions and solve problems, including actions that will reduce our carbon dioxide emissions.

Will we transform into a world powered by energy from renewable sources or will we remain reliant on fossil fuels? It's time to seek solutions and learn the value of thinking globally and acting locally. Read the next chapter to see how you can be part of the solution.

? ESSENTIAL QUESTION

Now it's time to consider and discuss the Essential Question:
How has human activity affected the earth's climate? How do we know?

Black Carbon

Glaciers have a bright, white surface, which means they reflect most of the sunlight hitting them instead of absorbing it. This helps keep temperatures in the polar regions cool. But burning fossil fuels creates black carbon, which settles as a visible layer of black soot on the glaciers. When that happens, glaciers absorb more sunlight and melt more quickly. How does this impact the water level of the world's oceans? What happens to animals that live on the ice? How could this contribute to raising the earth's temperature?

MEASURE AIR POLLUTANTS

IDEAS FOR SUPPLIES
index cards ✳ petroleum jelly

How do we know what's in the air? There are a lot of things in the air, including pollen, dust, germs, and gases. Dirty air that is full of **pollutants** is called polluted air. Air pollution is one of the consequences of burning fossil fuels. Learn how to test the air and collect and analyze data with this experiment.

1 Brainstorm three to five places to test for air pollution. Some ideas include your bedroom, the refrigerator, or your mailbox. Start a scientific method worksheet in your science journal and record your predictions for which areas you think are most impacted by air pollution.

2 Label an index card for each area. Smear a layer of petroleum jelly in the middle of the index cards and tape each card to its location.

3 Check your cards every two days for six days. In your science journal, record your observations from each location using a chart like this to keep track of your data.

Location	Initial Observation	Observation Day 2	Observation Day 4	Observation Day 6

GIANTS OF SCIENCE

Michael Faraday

In the 1700s and 1800s, we knew how to get energy from wind and water, but we didn't know how to turn it into electricity. Michael Faraday (1791–1867) discovered **electromagnetic conduction** in 1831. His discovery, along with others, made it possible to generate massive amounts of electricity from wind and water. Today, we have the potential to use wind, water, and other renewables to provide a constant stream of electricity to power our lives.

4 Which location had the most air pollution? Why? What could you do to improve the quality of the air in that area?

TRY THIS: This experiment explored visible air pollution, but what types of pollution may be invisible to our eyes? Is carbon dioxide a pollutant? Is carbon dioxide visible? Some of the worst air pollution in the world exists in China. With an adult's permission, use the Internet to find images of this country. What does it look like? Can you see the air pollution? How are people trying to keep themselves healthy?

pollutant: a substance that is harmful to the environment.

electromagnetic conduction: the use of a magnet to create electric energy.

WORDS 2 KNOW

COOL CONCEPT

The Great Pacific Garbage Patch is one of the largest concentrations of microscopic particles of plastic floating in the ocean. Although some estimates say it's the size of Texas, this trillion-particle patch is not visible from satellites because the pieces are so small.

Burning one gallon of gasoline releases 20 pounds of carbon dioxide. In the United States, we use 358,000,000 gallons of oil and gas every day for transportation. We all use transportation—cars, bikes, trains, buses, airplanes, and our own bodies. How much energy does your family use for transportation? How much carbon dioxide does your family release?

1 Ask a parent how many gallons of gas your family uses in one week for transportation. Record this amount in your science journal.

2 Based on your family's weekly use, how many gallons are used each year? There are 52 weeks in one year. Multiply your weekly use by 52 to get the gallons of gas used in one year.

weekly gas usage × 52 weeks = yearly gas usage

3 Multiply your yearly use by 20 pounds. This is your family's carbon dioxide emission, or the amount released, for transportation.

yearly gas usage × 20 pounds = CO_2 emissions per year

4 In your science journal, brainstorm ways to reduce your transportation CO_2 emissions. Are there times you could use your bike or walk? Do you ever ride the bus or subway? Do you carpool?

TRY THIS: Identify other activities that use energy. Audit your consumption of meat, hours of light bulbs turned on in your room, or hours of electronic devices charging. Which behaviors can you change?

LIGHT OVER TIME

IDEAS FOR SUPPLIES
*something to read * candle * lamp * overhead light * flashlight*

One of the most obvious uses for energy is light. What would your life be like without light? Would you go to bed earlier? Would you be able to read as many books? During the course of human history, we've searched for better and better ways to provide ourselves with light. Let's compare and contrast light from different sources. As you observe the quality of each light, think about points in history when there was no such thing as electricity or light bulbs.

Caution: Have an adult help you with the candle!

1 Make a table in your science journal listing all the light sources. Start a scientific method worksheet and make predictions about the quality of each source of light.

2 Have an adult light a candle. Read a couple of pages from a book or magazine using the candlelight. Write down your experience using this type of light. Would you want to use it again?

3 Blow out the candle and read your book using a lamp, an overhead light, and a flashlight. What do you think of these sources of light? Record your observations.

THINK ABOUT IT: Which was the best type of light to read by? Were any of the lights hard to read with? Can a light be both good for the environment and good for your eyes?

CARBON IN THE AIR

IDEAS FOR SUPPLIES
*matches * glass plate*

When we burn wood, coal, natural gas, or oil we release carbon dioxide into the air. Carbon dioxide is a colorless and odorless gas, so what proof is there of this release? In this experiment, you will burn a match to see if we can provide visual evidence of the release of carbon. What if we could see all the carbon we released into the air every day?

Caution: This activity requires the help of an adult.

1 Start a scientific method worksheet in your science journal. What will happen when you hold a burning match under a glass plate?

2 Place the glass plate on the counter so that the plate hangs over the edge of the counter by 2 or 3 inches.

3 With an adult, light the match and hold it under the edge of the plate for a few seconds before blowing it out. Can you see or smell anything on the spot where you held the burning match? Record your observations.

4 Once the plate has cooled, touch the area where you held the match. What does it feel like? Record your observations.

THINK ABOUT IT: Next time you roast marshmallows around a campfire, notice what happens to the wood as it burns. What does your marshmallow look like if it catches fire? When the campfire is out, what do the bits of burned wood look like? What do you know about the burned parts of the marshmallow and the wood?

CHAPTER 6
DOWNLOAD YOUR FUTURE

Life on Spaceship Earth is constantly changing. What was it like 10,000 years ago? The Ice Age was ending and humans lived a nomadic life, moving constantly in search of animals to hunt and plants to gather. As our climate warmed up, we adapted. We learned to grow food and raise animals. We changed from hunting and gathering to a society based on agriculture.

Fast forward to the 1700s and the beginning of the Industrial Revolution. This is when many people moved from agriculture to industry and traded farms and forests for factories. All of these changes altered our relationship to the natural world. Since then, human activity has added so much greenhouse gas in a short period of time that scientists worry about the lasting effects on wildlife, **habitats**, and the health of humans.

nomadic: moving from place to place to find food.

habitat: the natural area where a plant or an animal lives.

WORDS2KNOW

? ESSENTIAL QUESTION

What inspires people to change their energy habits? What can you do to help the planet?

WORDS 2 KNOW

efficient: wasting as little energy as possible.

civilization: a community of people that is advanced in art, science, and government.

conservation: to use something carefully, so it doesn't get used up.

Humans have accomplished many great things, including flight, walking on the moon, and creating the Internet. Through ingenuity and progress we have shaped the present, and now we must use that same ingenuity to shape the future. We are all responsible for making positive changes to keep Spaceship Earth a healthy place to live.

Energy Inventions

How do we use energy on Spaceship Earth? What do we use to light our homes, cook our food, and power our cars? Could we be more **efficient** in our use of energy?

Human **civilization** is full of inventions, from railroads that connect the east and west coasts to modern-day cell phones that connect people all over the world. Many inventions relate to energy and how we use it. As we understand more about the human impact on climate change, we can use our ingenuity to invent products that conserve energy.

What is the difference between efficiency and conservation?

PS

"Change Your Ways"

Watch 12-year-old Severn Cullis-Suzuki speak powerfully about her wishes and fears at the Rio Earth Summit. This speech gave her the title, "Girl Who Silenced the World for 5 Minutes."

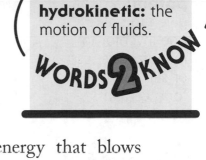

hydrokinetic: the motion of fluids.

WORDS 2 KNOW

We have designed batteries that enable cars to run on electricity instead of gasoline. We have invented concentrated solar power plants that can power 140,000 homes from the sun. Have you ever heard of a wind farm? Instead of vegetables, wind farms produce electricity by harnessing energy that blows naturally. Do an online image search for the word **hydrokinetic** and you'll find lots of inventions that are being developed to create electricity from the waves and tides of the ocean.

What powers your classroom? More than 3,700 schools in the United States currently have solar panels that collect energy from the sun and use it to keep classrooms bright and warm. Maybe your school will be next!

All of these inventions were created by people, including kids, who saw the need for new ways of making and using energy. Scientists, thinkers, mathematicians, moms, dads, and grandparents have put their heads together to engineer solutions. Let's explore some of the people designing solutions to address global climate change.

COOL CONCEPT

An Air Force base in Nevada has saved $83,000 a month since it switched to using solar energy produced on site.

Never Too Young or Too Old

Kids around the globe are taking positive community actions to protect the air, water, and land on Spaceship Earth. In the United States, the President's Environmental Youth Award is one of the highest honors to recognize the efforts of young people to slow climate change and protect the environment. Winners are given a certificate of recognition from the Environmental Protection Agency. This award recognizes young people who are taking positive community action to protect our shared resources.

One of the award winners, Deepika Kurup, developed a water purifying system that uses solar energy. She is currently getting a **patent** for her invention, which will help people around the world use the sun to create safe drinking water.

Kurup got to meet President Barack Obama and share her invention at the White House Science Fair.

Severn Cullis-Suzuki is a Canadian environmental activist who started her work on climate change in 1988 at the age of 9. She organized a group of friends and created the Environmental Children's Organization (ECO). ECO is dedicated to teaching others about environmental issues, such as how climate change impacts plants and animals.

Feeling as though you can't save the climate alone? Join with friends such as this group of 21 elementary students in Oklahoma. This team came together to rebuild the habitat that was destroyed near their school. All the students worked together with teachers to create a new living ecosystem laboratory in their own back yard. Their project is called "Beyond the Classroom: Where Have All the Flowers and Birds Gone?"

Campaigning, marching, walking, singing, tweeting, posting, photographing—all of these actions were part of the People's Climate March in September 2014. This weekend event consisted of 2,600 events in more than 162 countries. Kids, activists, parents, scientists, college students, and media brought attention to the impact of human actions on the earth's climate. The rally was in preparation for the gathering of the United Nations' climate summit.

The People's Climate March showed how people from diverse cultures can come together to change our future.

You Matter? iMatter!

Want to join the conversation? The iMatter campaign was started by 13-year-old Alec Loorz as a way to share stories and connect with other people concerned about the environment. The iMatter campaign incorporates videos, training, and digital storytelling to encourage children to learn more about their own actions.

Most Americans search for the term *global warming* rather than *climate change* when looking for information online about our changing climate. Why? Do you think this is a more accurate way of thinking about it?

COOL CONCEPT

President Obama is leading a commitment to stop climate change. He created the Climate Action Plan in June 2013 to commit the United States to reducing carbon emissions. The United States is the second-largest producer of carbon dioxide in the world, right behind China. Part of the Climate Action Plan focuses on getting companies to reduce carbon emissions. That means involving big factories and industries, including the trucks and ships that carry supplies around our country.

Like the Great Wall of China, China's air pollution is often visible from space.

Reinventing Our Future

It may seem like a big thing to slow climate change, but humans are pretty good at tackling big projects. We sent a robot to Mars! Reimagining and creating new products is an important part of changing everyday behavior and reducing greenhouse gas emissions.

In London, they are doing just that—implementing a small change to address a big issue. London's famous bright red telephone boxes have fallen out of use because everyone now has cell phones. What do Londoners need instead of public telephones? Charging stations!

Inspiration

Get inspired with this "What's Possible" video created by three moms. The video highlights the need for us to understand global warming and for all of us, from friends and families to schools and leaders, to act.

rural: areas in the countryside.

The city is painting the old red boxes the color green and adding solar panels to the roofs to create charging stations. Now you can plug in your cell phone, tablet, camera, or other device and power them from the sun, right on the streets of London. Making red telephone boxes "go green" is one small way to help slow climate change. And it shows how an outdated invention can be transformed for a new, clean-energy purpose.

"Going green" is the term used to describe changes that help improve our environment and climate.

Food is another opportunity for us to change our behaviors. The majority of the food we eat is grown on farms in **rural** areas. Farms can take up many hundreds and thousands of acres of land and may require specific climates. In a modern world, what invention could we come up with to improve our 12,000-year-old history of farming?

How about **vertical farming**? Vertical farms are just like they sound, farms that stretch up in the sky. Architects are working with planners and farmers to create spaces on the sides of buildings to grow food. Vertical farms allow for more sunlight for plants and a flow of water from one garden to another.

Vertical farming reshapes communities. People learn to grow and eat local food, and new jobs are created in urban areas.

Cleanup on Aisle Earth

vertical farming: growing food on vertical surfaces such as buildings or skyscrapers.

incinerator: a large furnace used to burn trash.

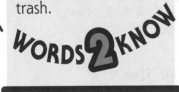

Another way people are working to slow climate change is by finding better ways to deal with waste. In the United States, most of the garbage goes to landfills or **incinerators**. Both landfills and incinerators contribute to global warming. As garbage rots, it not only adds greenhouse gases to our atmosphere, it also contributes other harmful pollutants to our air, land, and water. What else can we do with our garbage?

The largest indoor vertical farm in the United States is in a 90,000-square-foot warehouse in Illinois. Transformed from rubble, the warehouse now houses plots that grow herbs and plants to feed the local community.

More than 40 percent of the trash we throw away could be recycled. Much of our trash is food waste that could be composted.

compost: to recycle food scraps and vegetation and put them back in the soil.

WORDS 2 KNOW

A company called BigBelly has redesigned the way trash cans look and function—using solar energy. Instead of a round, open basket that lets trash fly out, they re-imagined a bin with a lever that keeps the trash in! The trash can also uses solar energy to compact the trash. The technology in these trash bins, which are in more than 11 states and in three countries, helps reduce the amount of trash on the streets or in landfills. All of these actions combined help us reduce the release of methane.

Paper, Plastic, or Cloth?

Each year, an estimated 500 billion to 1 trillion plastic bags are consumed worldwide. That's more than 1 million plastic bags used per minute! Next time you go grocery shopping, bring a reusable bag. Both plastic and paper bags require energy to be produced. Much of that energy releases greenhouse gases. Also, plastic bags can take up to 500 years to decompose.

GIANTS OF SCIENCE

Sylvia Earle

Sylvia Earle (1935–present) knows just how important our oceans are. As a marine biologist, she has spent 7,000 hours underwater! That's 291 days of her life. As the first female chief scientist for the U.S. National Oceanic and Atmospheric Administration, she was a role model for other women who want to explore oceans. Her explorations have helped us to define conservation efforts that address global warming. The documentary *Mission Blue* showcases her efforts to create and protect marine sanctuaries around the world.

Much of the plastic we throw out never makes it to a landfill or incinerator—it ends up in our oceans. Boyan Slat, a Dutch teenager, was concerned that there was more plastic than fish in the ocean.

He designed a simple technology for cleaning up the plastic in the ocean. Known as the Ocean Cleanup Array, this technology uses the ocean currents and V-shaped floating "arms" to capture plastics on the surface of the ocean. Organisms are able to go under the arms and avoid getting caught. By cleaning up the oceans, especially of plastics, we make it easier for the oceans to support life and absorb carbon dioxide.

COOL CONCEPT

The ocean is more than just a home to marine species. It provides food and medicines to people around the world, serves as a highway for the transportation of goods and people, and plays a role in supporting local economies.

Teaching and Learning About Climate Change

carbon footprint: the total amount of carbon dioxide and other greenhouse gases emitted over the full life cycle of a product or service, or by a person or family in a year.

WORDS 2 KNOW

Students across the country are teaming up to shrink the **carbon footprints** of their schools. Some of the following steps are local actions you can take to reduce your energy use and decrease greenhouse gas emissions. Create a "green team" of parents, teachers, and students and get started!

- **Recycling program:** No need to fill up our landfills with cans, bottles, and paper! Recycle everything possible.

- **Composting program:** When you don't eat that broccoli or peanut butter and jelly sandwich, do you throw it in the trash? Ask your school to start composting. Putting food waste back into the earth helps replenish nutrients in the soil.

- **School garden:** Once you start composting, have your school or classroom plant a garden. The garden can help you learn about energy and even grow food for school lunches.

- **Plant trees:** Did you know that planting trees is one of the easiest ways to help clean our air and fight climate change? You can plant trees in your school's playground and outside areas. One tree can absorb nearly 1 ton of carbon dioxide in its lifetime.

- **Energy efficient lighting:** Research what light bulbs are used in your school. Create a campaign for your school to change the light bulbs to more efficient ones. Many schools still use old fluorescent light bulbs that are less efficient than newly designed light bulbs.

Costa Rica

Since the end of WWII, nearly 80 percent of Costa Rica's forests have been cleared. But the "I Dare You To Plant A Tree" campaign, led by sustainable developer Alejandro Castro-Alfaro, is changing that story. In 2007, nearly 6,300,000 trees were planted. Tree by tree, Costa Rican people and organizations are helping to reforest the country.

- **Water-efficient bathroom sinks and toilets:** Each student in your school goes to the bathroom at least once a day. That uses a lot of water. Start a campaign to have automatic water sinks and toilets installed so you can reduce the amount of water used.

- **Large windows:** One easy way to help conserve energy is to make sure that classrooms and common spaces have daylight.

- **Smart thermostats:** These can show the actual temperature in your classroom and help regulate temperatures in your school. They can also work on timers so the heat or air conditioning isn't on during the evenings or weekends.

- **Have class outside!**

Schools around the country are starting composting programs. Some programs reduce the garbage that goes to a landfill by 85 percent!

PS Green Ambassadors

Explore how these students from across the country are helping their schools and community go green. The Green Ambassadors program works with students and teachers to implement green changes. Watch this video to get inspired.

Careers That Shape Our Planet

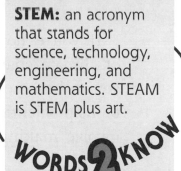

STEM: an acronym that stands for science, technology, engineering, and mathematics. STEAM is STEM plus art.

WORDS 2 KNOW

Have you ever heard of the term "green jobs?" It refers to jobs that help protect our environment and our earth. Many of these green jobs involve subjects such as science, technology, engineering, math, and art. You might have heard these subjects called the **STEM** or STEAM subjects.

The world needs kids like you to get involved as scientists, engineers, designers, and inventors.

COOL CONCEPT

Many of us have heard of solar, wind, or water power. What about converting algae to biofuel or heating water underground with geothermal technology? Check out these short videos on different renewable energy sources. The videos explore what they are and how the technology works.

107

There are many different jobs involved in studying and slowing climate change. Here's a list of energy and STEAM careers related to the climate. Work with a parent to research these jobs online.

- oceanographer
- meteorologist
- ecologist
- geologist
- sustainable development director
- green building contractor
- home energy auditor
- climate change researcher
- air quality specialists
- climate change community organizer
- carbon management consultant
- climate program officer

If you're not a scientist yet but want to help track the impact of climate change, there are plenty of **citizen science** projects for you to become involved in. These are projects done by local people to help scientists gather and analyze data. Many of these projects involve making observations or collecting data.

From tracking bird migration to taking pictures underwater, these projects help scientists solve problems.

citizen science: the involvement of everyday people in scientific activities or projects.

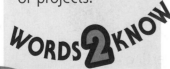

COOL CONCEPT

What happens in one part of the globe has an effect on other locations. When a volcano erupts in Greenland, the ash disrupts airplanes across Europe. Warming waters in the Indian Ocean change the fishing off the coast of Africa. Citizen scientists play a large role in collecting data from all around the globe to help us understand what is happening.

Counting Birds

The Great Backyard Bird Count, hosted by the Cornell Lab of Ornithology and National Audubon Society, is an annual project that examines birds. Bird migration can tell us a lot about climate change. As the temperatures get warmer, migration patterns change. The data gathered by ordinary citizens during a four-day count helps scientists better understand the impacts of climate change. You can view the data from previous years.

The Future is Yours

Human activity is changing our planet. Are we making changes to improve, maintain, and care for the systems that support life on Spaceship Earth? Or are we damaging the very systems that we rely on for our existence?

American scientist Margaret Mead once said, "Never doubt that a small group of thoughtful, committed citizens can change the world; indeed, it's the only thing that ever has." What do you think she meant? Think globally about how we are impacting our planet with our choices, and act locally to be part of the solution.

? **ESSENTIAL QUESTION**

Now it's time to consider and discuss the Essential Question: What inspires people to change their energy habits? What can you do to help the planet?

PLANT TREES IN YOUR COMMUNITY

IDEAS FOR SUPPLIES
recycled material for fliers ✳ drawing materials ✳ seeds or a tree

You've learned in this book that plants are critical to the balance of gases in our atmosphere because they absorb carbon dioxide and release oxygen. Planting a tree is an easy and important part of fighting climate change. With your family and friends, organize a campaign to plant trees in your neighborhood!

1 Create a flyer about planting trees in your neighborhood or school using markers or crayons and recycled materials. Include some of the facts you have learned about global warming. List some of the other benefits trees provide—shade, climbing opportunities, and beauty. Encourage people to become part of the solution!

2 With an adult's permission, go online to research what types of trees grow best in your region. What type of soil do different trees need to thrive? Does it get very cold in the winter? How long is your growing season? Be sure to give your trees the best possible start by choosing the right varieties.

3 With an adult, order your 10 free trees from the Arbor Foundation or purchase trees from a local arbor or gardening center.

COOL CONCEPT

You can join the Arbor Foundation for $15 a year and get 10 free trees for your neighborhood.

4 In your science journal, make a record of when and where you plant the trees. Come up with a plan to care for them as they grow. Trees need regular watering during the first year after planting.

TRY THIS: Track the growth of the new trees. Measure their height and width every month and record the measurements in your science journal. Are some trees growing faster than others? Why? Is the soil different? Are they getting more or less sun? Track the growth during a year and share your results with the people who helped you plant the trees. How big do you think they'll be in five years? Ten years?

GIANTS OF SCIENCE

Your Name Here

What will you do to impact climate change?

WRITE A LETTER TO THE MAYOR

Every day, our government officials at both the state and national levels make decisions that impact climate change. Make sure your voice is heard!

1 Ask an adult to help you find the name and address of your mayor. You can usually find this information online. A mayor is a government official who leads a city or town. If your town doesn't have a mayor, write to your governor, who is the leader of your state. Write the name and address on the envelope.

2 Make a list in your science journal of the points you want to include in your letter. What commitments can you make to help stop climate change? What information about climate change can you share with the elected official? What do you want the mayor to do?

3 Draft your letter. Note that elected officials appreciate and respond to original letters. If you need help writing your letter, look at the sample language on the next page as a starting point.

4 Revise your letter. Make sure you use correct grammar and spelling! Have a parent read your letter, and revise again if necessary.

5 Fold your letter neatly and put it in the envelope. Put a stamp on it and send it off in the mail.

Dear Mayor _____,

I am writing to let you know that I have learned about climate change and want to help. I recently read *Climate Change: Discover How It Impacts Spaceship Earth* by Joshua Sneideman and Erin Twamley and realize that climate change is impacting my home, my friends, and our community. Climate change is impacting me because _____. I have committed to helping stop climate change by _____.

I am writing to you to ask for your help. I would like you to consider signing the U.S. Mayors Climate Protection Agreement that has been signed by nearly 400 of your colleagues. It's a 12-step program that sets reasonable goals for your city to reduce carbon dioxide emissions to below what the levels were in 1990.

Please join these other mayors in being leaders in the fight to stop climate change. The kids of the world are depending on you.

Sincerely,

_____,

Age _____

TRY THIS: Research other organizations that officials can join or sign a pledge of support for. Write to other government leaders encouraging them to show support for slowing climate change.

Do you know how much food you waste in a day? Our food waste contributes to climate change. The production of food requires the use of energy. When we throw food away we are wasting energy and food. How can you change your behaviors to help reduce waste? Try this activity for a day or a week and find out.

1 Start a scientific method worksheet in your science journal. Create a Waste Tracking Chart. How much food does your family waste each week?

2 After every meal or snack, record what you don't eat. Write down how much food you wasted and how you threw it away. Did it go in the trash? The compost bin? Did you feed it to the dog under the table? Ask an adult to help you estimate the cost of the wasted food.

3 At the end of the week, total your findings. How much food did you waste during a week? How much money did it cost? Was it more or less than you thought it would be? At this rate how much food do you waste in a year?

TRY THIS: How can you reduce food waste each day? Post a list of your ideas on the refrigerator so you'll be reminded not to waste food. How can your community waste less food? Find out what people are doing in your area with extra food.

COOL CONCEPT

The United States has only 5 percent of the world's population, but contributes 22 percent of the world's carbon emissions.

absorb: to soak up.

acids: chemical substances.

adapt: to change to survive in new or different conditions.

agriculture: growing crops and raising animals for food.

algae: a plant-like organism that turns light into energy. Algae does not have leaves or roots.

altitude: the height of land above the level of the sea. Also called *elevation*.

analyze: to study and examine.

atmosphere: the mixture of gases surrounding a planet.

atmospheric pressure: the weight of all the air pressing down on an area.

atom: the smallest particle of an element.

axis: the imaginary line through the North and South Poles that the earth rotates around.

bacteria: tiny microorganisms that live in animals, plants, soil, and water.

balance: when the different parts of something, such as in the environment or the climate, are distributed in the right amounts so that the whole system works and can keep working.

biofuel: fuel made from living matter, such as plants.

boreal forest: a northern forest filled mostly with conifers, which are trees with needles that produce cones. Most conifers are evergreens that do not lose their leaves each year.

carbon cycle: the movement of carbon through the earth's ecosystems.

carbon dioxide: a combination of carbon and oxygen that is formed by the burning of fossil fuels, the rotting of plants and animals, and the breathing out of animals or humans.

carbon footprint: the total amount of carbon dioxide and other greenhouse gases emitted over the full life cycle of a product or service, or by a person or family in a year.

celestial body: a star, planet, moon, or object in the sky.

citizen science: the involvement of everyday people in scientific activities or projects.

civilization: a community of people that is advanced in art, science, and government.

climate: the prevailing weather conditions of a region throughout the year, averaged over a series of years. These conditions include temperature, air pressure, humidity, precipitation, winds, sunshine, and cloudiness.

climate change: a change in the long-term average weather patterns of a place.

climatologist: a scientist who studies the climate.

colony: a population of plants or animals of one species that lives in a particular place.

compost: to recycle food scraps and vegetation and put them back in the soil.

compress: to squeeze a material very tightly.

conclusion: an opinion or decision that is formed after a period of thought or research.

condense: when a gas cools down and changes into a liquid.

conservation: to use something carefully, so it doesn't get used up.

consumption: using a resource.

convection current: the movement of hot air rising and cold air sinking.

coral band: a layer added each year to coral reefs.

coral bleaching: a sign of poor health in coral that happens when algae in the coral die or lose their color.

coral reef: an underwater ecosystem made by coral.

core: the center of an object.

cryosphere: the frozen areas of the earth, including glaciers.

data: information, usually measured in the form of numbers, that can be processed by a computer.

decompose: to rot or decay.

deforestation: the clearing of the forests.

GLOSSARY

dendrochronologist: a scientist who studies tree rings.

dense: how tightly the matter in an object is packed.

dissolve: when molecules of one substance get mixed into the molecules of another substance.

diverse: a large variety.

drought: a long period of time without rain.

ecosystem: a community of living and nonliving things and their environment. Living things are plants, animals, and insects. Nonliving things are soil, rocks, and water.

efficient: wasting as little energy as possible.

electromagnetic conduction: the use of a magnet to create electric energy.

electromagnetic waves: waves that can travel through the emptiness of space.

element: a substance whose atoms are all the same. Examples include gold, oxygen, nitrogen, and carbon.

elliptical: shaped like an ellipse, or an oval.

emission: something sent or given off, such as smoke, gas, heat, or light.

enzyme: a substance in an organism used to speed up the rate of chemical reactions.

equilibrium: to be in balance.

evaporate: when a liquid heats up and changes into a gas.

evolve: to gradually develop through time and become more complex.

excess: more than the normal amount.

food chain: a community of animals and plants where each is eaten by another higher up in the chain.

fossil: the remains or traces of ancient plants or animals left in rock.

fossil fuels: coal, oil, and natural gas. These energy sources come from the fossils of plants and microorganisms that lived millions of years ago.

fossil record: a record of information of the past that a collection of fossils can provide.

fusion: when the nucleus of one atom combines with the nucleus of another atom, which releases energy.

geologist: a scientist who studies the history, structure, and origin of the earth.

glaciologist: a scientist who studies glaciers.

global warming: an increase in the average temperature of the earth's atmosphere.

greenhouse effect: when gases in the atmosphere permit sunlight to pass through but then trap heat, causing the warming of the earth's environment.

greenhouse gas: a gas in the atmosphere that traps heat. We need some greenhouse gases, but too many trap too much heat.

habitable zone: the region at a distance from a star where liquid water is likely to exist.

habitat: the natural area where a plant or an animal lives.

heat-trapping gas: a gas, such as carbon dioxide, water vapor, or methane, that absorbs and stores heat.

helium: a light gas often used to fill balloons. It is the most abundant element after hydrogen.

hemisphere: half of the earth. Above the equator is called the Northern Hemisphere and below is the Southern Hemisphere.

hydrogen: the simplest and most abundant element in the universe.

hydrokinetic: the motion of fluids.

ice core: a sample of ice taken out of glacier, used to study climate.

impact: an effect or influence.

incinerator: a large furnace used to burn trash.

industrialization: when there is a lot of manufacturing, with products made by machines in large factories.

GLOSSARY

Industrial Revolution: a period of time beginning in the late 1700s when people started using machines to make things in large factories.

infrared: an invisible type of light with a longer wavelength than visible light, which can also be felt as heat.

inhabitant: a person or animal that lives in a particular place.

interconnected: when two or more things have an impact on each other.

lens: a clear, curved piece of glass or plastic that is used in eyeglasses, cameras, and telescopes to make things look clearer or bigger.

limestone: a kind of rock that forms from the skeletons and shells of sea creatures.

litmus paper: a special paper used to test whether a substance is an acid or base.

mass: the amount of matter in an object.

Mesozoic Era: a period of time from about 252 to 66 million years ago, when dinosaurs roamed the earth.

meteorology: the study of weather and climate.

methane: a greenhouse gas that is colorless and odorless, composed of carbon and hydrogen.

microfossil: a tiny fossil that can be seen only with a microscope.

microorganism: a living thing that is so small it can be seen only with a microscope. Also called a microbe.

molecule: a group of atoms bound together to form a new substance. Examples include carbon dioxide (CO_2), one carbon atom and two oxygen atoms, and water (H_2O), two hydrogen atoms and one oxygen atom.

natural resource: something found in nature that is useful to humans, such as water to drink, trees to burn, and fish to eat.

nitrogen: the most common gas in the earth's atmosphere.

nomadic: moving from place to place to find food.

nonrenewable: resources that can be used up, that we can't make more of, such as oil.

nuclear reaction: when atoms fuse together or split apart. This releases a large amount of energy.

nucleus: the center of an atom. Plural is nuclei.

nutrients: substances in food and soil that living things need to live and grow.

ocean acidification: when oceans absorb too much carbon dioxide and become more acidic.

orbit: a repeating path that circles around something else.

organism: any living thing, such as a plant or animal.

oxygen: a gas in the atmosphere that people and animals need to breathe to stay alive.

paleontologist: a scientist who studies fossils.

patent: a right given to only one inventor to manufacture, use, or sell an invention for a certain number of years.

permafrost: in far northern areas, the ground underneath the top layer of soil that is permanently frozen.

photoelectric effect: the creation of an electric current after exposure to light.

photosynthesis: the process in which plants use sunlight, water, and carbon dioxide to create energy.

pollutant: a substance that is harmful to the environment.

precipitation: condensed water vapor that falls to the earth's surface in the form of rain, snow, sleet, or hail.

primary: the main source of something.

recyclable: something that can be recycled by shredding, squashing, pulping, or melting to use the materials to create new products.

regulate: to control something.

GLOSSARY

renewable energy: a form of energy that doesn't get used up, including the energy of the sun and the wind.

respiratory system: the parts of the body used to breathe.

rotation: turning around a fixed point.

rural: areas in the countryside.

scientific inquiry: an approach to teaching and learning science based on questions, experiments, and evaluation of data.

scientific instrument: a tool or device used in science experiments.

sea level: the level of the surface of the sea.

sedimentary layer: a layer of rock formed from the compression of sediments, the remains of plants and animals, or from the evaporation of seawater.

solar panel: a device used to capture sunlight and convert it to usable energy.

solar power: energy from the sun converted to electricity.

solar system: the collection of eight planets, moons, and other celestial bodies that orbit the sun.

species: a group of living things that are closely related and look similar.

speed of light: the speed at which light travels.

starch: a type of nutrient found in certain foods, such as bread, potatoes, and rice.

STEM: an acronym that stands for science, technology, engineering, and mathematics. STEAM is STEM plus art.

symbiotic: the relationship between two different kinds of living things that depend on each other.

system: a set of connected parts working together.

theory: an explanation of how or why something happens that is accepted to be true.

tree rings: layers of wood inside a tree added each year as it grows.

trend: a particular direction or path.

universe: everything that exists, everywhere.

vacuum: a space that is empty.

vertical farming: growing food on vertical surfaces such as buildings or skyscrapers.

water cycle: the continuous movement of water from the earth to the clouds and back again.

water vapor: water as a gas, such as fog, steam, or mist.

wavelength: the distance from crest to crest in a series of waves.

Metric Equivalents

Use this chart to find the metric equivalents to the English measurements in this book. If you need to know a half measurement, divide by two. If you need to know twice the measurement, multiply by two. How do you find a quarter measurement? How do you find three times the measurement?

English	Metric
1 inch	2.5 centimeters
1 foot	30.5 centimeters
1 yard	0.9 meter
1 mile	1.6 kilometers
1 pound	0.5 kilogram
1 teaspoon	5 milliliters
1 tablespoon	15 milliliters
1 cup	237 milliliters

WEBSITES FOR KIDS

EPA Global Climate Change for Kids
epa.gov/climatechange/kids/index.html

NOAA for Kids
oceanservice.noaa.gov/kids

NASA's Climate Kids
climatekids.nasa.gov/nasa-research

Recycle City
epa.gov/recyclecity/mainmap.htm

Environmental Careers
ionfuture.org

**Interactive timeline of climate and
energy events throughout history**
abc.net.au/innovation/environment/cc_timeline.html

WEBSITES FOR EDUCATORS

Will Steger Foundation Climate Lessons
willstegerfoundation.org/climate-lessons-blog

NEED (National Energy Education Development) Project
need.org

Climate Literacy & Energy Awareness Network (CLEAN)
cleanet.org

NOAA Teaching Climate
climate.gov/teaching

Climate Change Education
ncse.com/climate

TED-Ed: A Guide to the Energy of the Earth
ed.ted.com/lessons/a-guide-to-the-energy-of-the-earth-joshua-m-sneideman

Energy Videos from the International Museum Network
sciencebeyondtheboundaries.com/EnergyVideos.html

QR CODE INDEX

Page 4: *youtube.com/watch?v=p86BPM1GV8M&feature=kp*

Page 9: *mathsisfun.com/data/graphs-index.html; nces.ed.gov/nceskids/createagraph/default.aspx; jmathpage.com/JIMSStatisticspage.html*

Page 23: *mars.jpl.nasa.gov/msl/multimedia/videos/index.cfm?v=49; space.com/27217-nasa-mars-maven-spacecraft-arrival.html*

Page 32: *ptaff.ca/soleil/?lang=en_CA*

Page 52: *changingthebalance.thinkport.org/molecules_move_greenhouse_gasesflash.html?iframe=true&width=810&height=510*

Page 55: *water.usgs.gov/edu/watercycle-kids-adv.html*

Page 67: *google.com/maps/views/streetview/oceans?gl=us*

Page 68: *iodp.tamu.edu/publicinfo/ship_stats.html*

Page 69: *ucl.ac.uk/GeolSci/micropal/radiolaria.html#cenozoic; nsf.gov/news/special_reports/science_nation/arcticlakes.jsp*

Page 70: *youtube.com/watch?v=vqicp4PvHrY*

Page 72: *youtube.com/watch?v=y0OKIbaXpvw&feature=youtu.be*

Page 73: *eospso.nasa.gov*

Page 75: *learnnc.org/lp/media/uploads/2008/06/pra53jan.jpg*

Page 79: *worldviewofglobalwarming.org/pages/glaciers.php*

Page 81: *nasa.gov/images/content/719286main1_2008_2012_printdata-673.jpg; epa.gov/climatechange/science/indicators/weather-climate/temperature.html*

Page 84: *esrl.noaa.gov/gmd/ccgg/trends/history.html*

Page 88: *eia.gov/todayinenergy/detail.cfm?id=11951*

Page 96: *youtube.com/watch?v=oJJGuIZVfLM*

Page 99: *imatteryouth.org*

Page 101: *youtube.com/watch?v=-vaajVtgRuI*

Page 107: *youngvoicesonclimatechange.com/movie_green-ambassadors.php; youtube.com/playlist?list=PLACD8E92715335CB2*

Page 109: *gbbc.birdsource.org/gbbcApps/maproom*

Page 110: *shop.arborday.org/memberships-ten-trees.aspx*

INDEX